GUIDE TO CASH MANAGEMENT

OTHER ECONOMIST BOOKS

Guide to Analysing Companies
Guide to Business Modelling
Guide to Business Planning
Guide to Economic Indicators
Guide to the European Union
Guide to Financial Management
Guide to Financial Markets
Guide to Hedge Funds
Guide to Investment Strategy
Guide to Management Ideas and Gurus
Guide to Managing Growth
Guide to Organisation Design
Guide to Project Management
Guide to Supply Chain Management
Numbers Guide
Style Guide

Book of Isms
Book of Obituaries
Brands and Branding
Business Consulting
Business Strategy
Buying Professional Services
The City
Coaching and Mentoring
Doing Business in China
Economics
Emerging Markets
Marketing
Megachange
Modern Warfare, Intelligence and Deterrence
Organisation Culture
Successful Strategy Execution
The World of Business

Directors: an A–Z Guide
Economics: an A–Z Guide
Investment: an A–Z Guide
Negotiation: an A–Z Guide

Pocket World in Figures

The
Economist

GUIDE TO CASH MANAGEMENT

How to avoid a business credit crunch

John Tennent

WILEY

John Wiley & Sons, Inc.

Published by John Wiley & Sons, Inc., Hoboken, New Jersey.
Published simultaneously in Canada.
Published in Great Britain and the rest of the world by Profile Books Ltd

For general information on our other products and services or for technical support,
please contact our Customer Care Department within the United States at
(800) 762-2974, outside the United States at (317) 572-3993 or fax (317) 572-4002.

Wiley also publishes its books in a variety of electronic formats. Some content that
appears in print may not be available in electronic books. For more information about
Wiley products, visit our web site at www.wiley.com.

Library of Congress Cataloging-in-Publication Data:

ISBN 978-1-118-09484-6 (cloth); ISBN 978-1-118-16659-8 (ebk);
ISBN 978-1-118-16657-4 (ebk); ISBN 978-1-118-16658-1 (ebk)

Printed in the United States of America

10 9 8 7 6 5 4 3 2 1

Contents

Preface

THE GLOBAL BANKING CRISIS and subsequent tightening of credit highlighted the importance of cash and cash flow to sustaining a business. Those that had ignored the warning signs and were subjected to stricter credit criteria soon found themselves in trouble.

This guide to cash management is designed to take you through the principles used to manage cash and cash flow and illustrate their practical application. It starts with some financial fundamentals and then covers forecasting, funding, working capital management, investment criteria and the utilisation of surpluses. Each chapter is written from an operational rather than a banking perspective. At the end is a glossary of the financial terms used in the book.

Most books are not just the work of the author but also incorporate contributions from many others. I am grateful to clients and colleagues at Corporate Edge who provided the opportunity to explore aspects of business, complete research and develop my thinking. In particular, I would like to thank Jonathan Crofts and Patrick Schmidt for reviewing the drafts and Profile Books for the help they gave me, particularly Stephen Brough, Penny Williams and Jonathan Harley.

Special thanks to my wife, Angela, and my two sons, William and George, who have supported my enthusiasm for writing, even on holidays. Also to my parents, particularly my father, a chartered accountant, who always encouraged my career, and was the author of a cash management book in 1976. While the fundamentals may not have changed, the technology with which to apply them is very different, as is the political and economic climate.

I would welcome feedback and can be contacted at this e-mail address: John-Tennent@CorporateEdge.co.uk

John Tennent
March 2012

Introduction

Cash management

To run a successful business requires effective management of a variety of resources that include all or some of the following: people, equipment, property, cash, a brand, products, services and inventory. Of all these resources cash is probably the most important. With sufficient cash a business has the ability to buy almost any of the other resources in which it may be deficient. Whether the purchase of that resource is worthwhile at the price required is another matter, but the purchase can still be made. All the resources other than cash have a value to a business that is dependent on their availability, utilisation, market demand and the prevailing economic climate. It is cash and only cash that maintains a constant value and can easily be turned into other assets or resources. This book explores the effective management of this most precious resource.

At a personal level we learn by experience the fundamentals of managing cash. We have a bank account and a monthly statement that tells us our cash balance and itemises all the receipts and payments. Intuitively we know that we must have more cash coming in than going out if we are to avoid debt. A cash crisis occurs when we have to make payments from a depleted bank account and find our borrowing limits have already been reached. In a business, few people have access to the type of cash information that we have at home. Therefore cash flow may appear to be an activity that can be forecast, analysed, monitored and managed by "someone in finance". However, there is both a legal and an operational responsibility for managing cash that extends across the whole of a business's management.

In some countries there is a legal responsibility based in insolvency law. For example in the UK it is an offence for directors to continue to trade if their company cannot pay its debts when they fall due. Directors have a duty to their staff and to their creditors to acknowledge when a business is in financial difficulty. Failure to act when evidence is available can lead to directors becoming personally liable for certain debts.

The operational responsibility requires everyone in a business to understand how their individual actions affect cash and to take responsibility for making changes that can improve its flow. However, many managers have a poor understanding of cash flow and any performance incentives often direct their energy to other aspects of the business such as sales volume or new business generation. Consequently, many businesses can become inefficient in their use of cash by tying up huge amounts in working capital and poorly utilised assets. The challenge is to raise awareness, responsibility and reward for improvements.

The starting point for surmounting this challenge is for managers and staff alike to have a sound knowledge of cash management. This includes an awareness of the signs of a looming cash crisis in both their own business and those of others with which they trade, as well as the skills to deal with the crisis before it becomes a disaster.

Cash and cash flow

It is not the amount of cash that a business has in its bank accounts that will make it successful; the role of management is to generate a financial return on the business activities that is substantially greater than an investor can achieve from other less risky investments such as a deposit account. Holding cash will not help achieve this objective. The focus of management is therefore to build a business that can generate a sustainable cash flow and deliver a superior return on investment for investors.

The difference between cash and cash flow can be illustrated by an analogy to the way water supplies are managed. A water company has an unpredictable supply of rain and thus holds a reservoir of water to meet demand. The size of the reservoir depends on the

FIG 1 **Cash and cash flow**

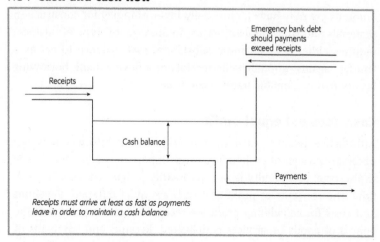

Emergency bank debt
should payments
exceed receipts

Receipts

Cash balance

Payments

*Receipts must arrive at least as fast as payments
leave in order to maintain a cash balance*

water company's ability to forecast two things: the supply of rain and customer demand. If daily supplies of rain consistently exceed daily demands for water, almost no reservoir is required.

If water represents cash, the amount of cash required in a business depends on the predictability of both the "supply" or receipts of cash from trading activities and the "demand" or payments of cash to suppliers and staff. Cash flow is the ability to generate a sufficient supply of cash so that a business is able to meet its demand for cash. The alternative is to have external investors who are prepared to fund any shortfall; but to encourage external investment, the management must demonstrate that the business can achieve a positive cash flow that will be sufficient to pay interest and ultimately enable repayment.

An example of a business with a highly predictable cash flow is a supermarket chain, where every day its customers pay over a vast amount of cash (or cash equivalents such as cheques and credit cards). The volume of the core food products that are sold is little affected by the economic climate and therefore the daily receipts from sales are easy to forecast. Payments to suppliers will usually be made after the cash has been received from customers, which could be up to two months or more after the goods were supplied. In these circumstances, the business needs to hold little cash. Contrast this with a house builder that makes a few irregular sales of large amounts yet may have almost daily invoices to pay for construction materials and subcontractor wages. To manage this type of business requires either a much more substantial cash balance to act as a "buffer" against unpredictable receipts or a flexible bank borrowing facility that will enable trade to continue.

Cash does not equal profit

Although a positive cash flow is critical to a business it is not necessarily a sign of profitability. More important is that the opposite is also true: profitability is not necessarily a sign of a positive cash flow. The concepts of profit and cash are quite different. Revenues and costs for calculating profit are recognised at the point that the benefit of goods or services is delivered. Receipts and payments of cash are recorded when money is transferred. Although the difference is in timing, the gap between when an event is recognised for profit purposes and when it is recognised for cash purposes can be long, as the following examples illustrate:

■ A customer buys goods on March 1st but pays for them on July 31st by taking five months' credit. For profit purposes the business would show the sale of the goods when they are delivered in March, but the bank account would not show the cash receipt until July. In the intervening period the business may well need to pay suppliers, staff and overhead costs, thus putting a strain on cash resources.

■ An example of an event when cash flow can be positive yet loss-making is a clothing retailer's end-of-season sale. The event may generate a lot of cash from customers, yet the items may be sold below cost and hence realise a loss.

■ A more extreme example is the purchase of production equipment that is expected to last ten years. The impact on cash will be substantial and negative at the point the equipment is purchased, yet the cost of this equipment for profit purposes will be spread over ten years using the process of depreciation. The cash to pay for the machine will ultimately come from the sale of the goods it produces. In this case, a long-term loan may be required to fund the purchase. The investors will be reliant on a sustainable business that can generate a positive cash flow from the equipment that will enable repayment.

These examples show that profit effects can differ from cash flow effects. Ultimately, in achieving a superior return on investment for its investors, a business will need to operate profitably and with a sustainable cash flow. If it cannot forecast both these attributes confidently, it will be difficult to attract external investment to carry the business through the mismatch in the timing of events.

A guide to cash management

The examples illustrate that the effective management of cash and more importantly cash flow depends on six critical factors:

- Cash flow forecasting of likely cash receipts and payments to ensure a business can meet its payment obligations as they fall due.
- Treasury management to establish funding lines with investors and banks (including effective control of borrowing facilities to enable the drawing down of cash for either a substantial asset purchase or working capital when short-term cash demand exceeds short-term cash supply).
- Efficiently managing day-to-day operations to minimise the amount of cash required to maintain and grow activities.
- Selecting appropriate investment opportunities that will result in an overall positive cash flow for the business.
- Monitoring the portfolio of products and services to ensure they are cash generative and not cash consuming, thereby managing the future viability of the business.
- Having a plan for managing surplus cash.

This book starts with an explanation of concepts and principles that are essential to understanding the way cash is used within a business and then looks at each of these factors.

1 Key concepts

WHATEVER THE FASHIONABLE BUSINESS topic of the day – globalisation, outsourcing, carbon emissions – the most enduring focus of all businesses is cash. Cash is probably the most important resource in running a successful business, and cash flow is crucial for sustaining the business activities. However, investors will measure and monitor a much wider range of attributes of the business in assessing its performance. These include indicators such as revenue, income (or profits), earnings, EBITDA (earnings before interest, tax, depreciation and amortisation), assets, working capital and leverage. Some of these have an indirect link to cash flow, but their effective management is no less important to the overall running of a successful business. When the results of an international company are reported in the media it is normally the profits or losses for the last 12 months that are the main focus. Debts, revenue and even executive pay will typically receive more coverage than either cash or cash flow. Therefore as cash flow management is developed in this book it is necessary to understand the ripple effects that actions will have on all aspects of the business. The main ingredient for achieving a strong cash flow is the effective management of all the other business resources being deployed, so a clear understanding of those resources is an integral part of understanding how to develop an effective cash flow.

This chapter covers a range of concepts and principles that define a successful business, identifies the main attributes of financial reporting and illustrates the way performance is measured by a range of stakeholders. See also *The Economist Guide to Financial Management*, which covers all these concepts and principles as well as others in more detail.

Business success

The goal of many businesses is to deliver a sustainable, superior return on investment (ROI). The return is the investors' reward for risking their money in the business. The concept is similar to a savings account where an amount of money is placed on deposit with a bank and the investor earns interest on it. A savings account is seen as low risk and consequently the return that the investor will make is similarly low.

$$\text{ROI for a savings account} \quad = \quad \frac{\text{Interest}}{\text{Investment}} \quad \%$$

Thus if a deposit of $1,000 is placed in a bank and the gross interest earned over a year is $30, the ROI is 3%.

For a business to be successful it needs to reward investors with a return higher than that of a savings account. The higher return is compensation for the greater investment risk as a consequence of the uncertainty in running a business. The return required might range from double to several times that from a savings account depending on the perceived level of risk, which will be related to factors such as the nature and maturity of the business.

The return in a business is derived from the profit it generates compared with the money invested to achieve that profit.

$$\text{ROI for a business} \quad = \quad \frac{\text{Profit}}{\text{Investment}} \quad \%$$

Thus if investors place $1,000 in a business and the operating profit over a year is $200, the ROI is 20%.

The business model

The business model in Figure 1.1 illustrates the financial structure of a business and the way cash flows around its various parts.

When a business is first established investors and others such as banks provide the initial capital in the form of cash to fund the business. There are then two main ways in which the cash can be spent:

■ Capital expenditure (often abbreviated to capex) on items that are known as fixed assets, which are intended to be used in

FIG 1.1 **A business model**

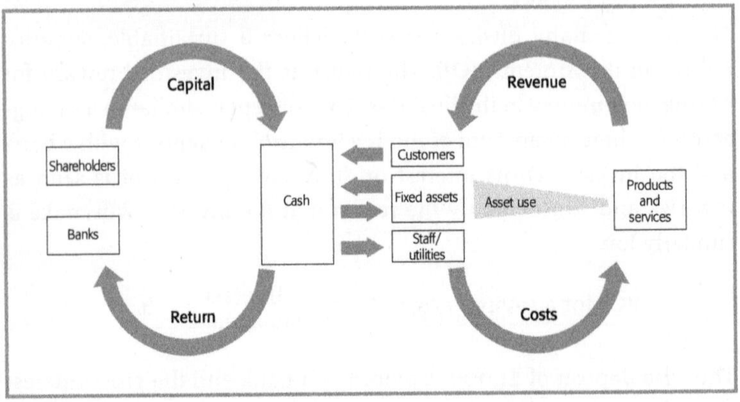

the business (rather than sold) and thus are typically in use for several years. Examples are buildings, machines and vehicles.

■ Operating expenditure (often abbreviated to opex) on items that will be consumed, used or sold in providing the products or services for customers or will be spent on administering these activities. Examples are utilities, staff costs and components.

Through expenditure on a mix of capital and operating resources and human endeavour, a business can provide the products and services that are sold to customers. Sales will either be on credit terms (as is usually the case with sales to other businesses) or for immediate payment (as is usually the case for sales to consumers). Credit sales will take time to turn into cash, even though the revenue will be recognised on the income statement at the point of sale.

A manufacturing business is likely to hold inventory of both raw materials and finished products. There may also be work in progress (products at various stages of construction or completion). Inventory and work in progress tie up cash, so keeping the levels of these items under control is an important part of cash efficiency.

For a business to be profitable, the cash received from selling products or services must, in the end, be greater than the cash required for their provision. This surplus can then be reinvested back in the business to fund its growth or returned to the investors.

Over time a business may accumulate fixed assets that are no longer required, become obsolete or are poorly utilised. In such cases they can be turned back into cash and perhaps provide some of the money required to fund new assets.

This business model provides the basis for all transactions that take place and therefore the basis on which they can be recorded, measured and monitored in order to achieve effective financial management. The most significant item in the process is cash, which has to be managed in conjunction with everything else and not in isolation. For example, understanding the inventory levels required for achieving good customer service or knowing the economic order quantities for achieving low-cost purchasing are advantageous to optimise profits, but an increase in inventory is potentially a drain on cash. There has to be a balance between these conflicts of optimising cash and optimising profit depending on the business situation and the prevailing operating environment.

Financial statements

There are three primary financial statements that are used to present the financial situation of a business covering the assets, liabilities, trading and cash flow:

- **The balance sheet or statement of financial position.** This is a snapshot of a business at a moment in time showing the assets that it owns, the liabilities that are owed and the money put in by investors. A balance sheet represents the items that should either provide a future benefit or have a future claim on the business. An alternative is to consider the balance sheet as a list of all the assets that investors' cash has been used to purchase and the liabilities incurred in running the business.

- **The income statement.** This is a statement of trading activity – also known as the profit and loss statement – that summarises the revenue earned and the costs incurred for a period. The costs comprise all the items that have been consumed or have been spent in earning the revenue and running the business. Ultimately, trading surpluses (or profits) will increase cash and any trading deficits (or losses) will reduce cash. However, the impact on cash will not necessarily arise at the same time as the surplus or deficit is recognised as, for example, revenue may be tied up in receivables, costs in payables and so on. In the long term, a profitable business will generate cash.

■ **The cash flow statement.** A summary of the cash received and paid over a period. This is effectively a summarised bank statement showing money in and money out.

When these three statements are reported they are normally historic, reporting what has happened in the past rather than what may happen in the future. Although this historic analysis may portray typical performance and be indicative of the future, creating a cash flow forecast, and understanding its alignment to budgets and business plans, is a far more useful management tool in avoiding a cash crisis (see Chapter 2). Clearly, it is easier to manage the future of a business by looking ahead rather than behind.

The three statements link together, with the balance sheet being a statement at a point in time and the income statement and cash flow summarising the activity over a period of time, typically a year.

Table 1.1 summarises the balance sheet and income statement; the cash flow statement is discussed in Chapter 2.

TABLE 1.1 **The balance sheet and income statement**

US term	UK term	Amount	Explanation
Balance sheet or statement of financial position			
Property, plant and equipment	Tangible fixed assets	150	Items that are owned and used in the business such as premises, vehicles and machines. These assets are depreciated to reflect their wearing out over time. The value in the balance sheet is known as the net book value after depreciation
Intangible assets	Intangible assets	100	Similar to tangible fixed assets except they are valuable rights and are usually paper-based, such as patents, trademarks and brands

US term	UK term	Amount	Explanation
Goodwill	Goodwill	50	A type of intangible asset that arises on the acquisition of a business. It represents the value of the acquisition over and above its specific net assets and covers items such as brand, reputation, customer base and employees
Current assets	Current assets		A collective term for the short-term assets that are likely to be converted into cash within one year
Inventory	Stock	50	Items ready or being constructed for sale, consisting of raw materials, work in progress and finished products
Receivables	Debtors	40	Amounts owed to the business from customers for sales it made on credit
Cash	Cash	10	The bank balance (and any physical cash held)
Total assets		400	
Current liabilities	Current liabilities		A collective term for the short-term liabilities that must be settled within one year
Payables	Creditors	30	Amounts owed to suppliers for products purchased on credit
Loans	Loans	120	Money borrowed from banks
Provisions	Provisions	60	A future obligation that is uncertain in amount and timing, such as the funding of a shortfall in a company pension fund
Common stock	Ordinary shares	100	The money raised by the business when it issued its shares
Reserves (retained earnings)	Reserves (retained profit)	90	Profits made by the business that have not been distributed to shareholders by way of dividends
Total liabilities		400	

Income statement

US term	UK term	Amount	Explanation
Revenue	Sales	300	The value of all products and services sold and delivered to customers

US term	UK term	Amount	Explanation
Cost of sales	Cost of sales	(260)	The costs involved in making and producing the products that have been sold, sometimes known as the cost of goods sold
Gross profit	Gross profit	40	Revenue less cost of sales gives gross profit
Selling, general and administration	Expenses	(15)	The overheads of the business that do not specifically relate to making or producing the products, such as rent, IT, accounting and other head-office costs
Operating income	Operating profit	25	Gross profit less expenses gives operating income
Interest	Interest	(5)	Interest charged on the business's borrowings
Income tax	Tax	(5)	Tax charged on the business's profits
Earnings	Earnings	15	The profit available for shareholders once all costs have been met

Financial principles

There are many financial principles underpinning the way business activities are accounted for in the two statements discussed above. This section focuses on the ones that will help in understanding the most important numbers and how they can be affected by management actions.

Revenue recognition

Revenue is recognised on the income statement when products or services are delivered to the customer. Importantly, this is not necessarily the same time that the cash is received. If a transaction takes place between two businesses, it is likely that the buyer will take a period of credit on the purchase so the cash will reach the seller 30–90 days after the products or services were provided. Sales made, for which cash has not been received, represent the receivables or debtors figure on the balance sheet.

For businesses that provide services such as travel (airlines and tour operators, for instance) or insurance, it is normal for the cash to be received in advance of customers receiving the benefits of their purchase. This is advantageous to cash flow, but it makes no difference to the timing of when revenue is recognised, as this is still based on the date that the products or services are delivered to the customer. In the case of insurance, the revenue is recognised in equal amounts over the period that cover is provided.

Another example of the way cash recognition is different from revenue recognition is in a mobile telecommunications business where a customer switches from a prepaid "pay as you go" deal to a post-paid contract. From a revenue-recognition perspective there would be no effect as connection revenue is recognised at the point a call is made (specifically when a call is terminated) or a text sent. However, from a cash perspective the effect is very different. In a prepaid deal the cash is received perhaps a month or two before a call is made. For a post-paid contract the cash will arrive perhaps a month or two after the call is made. This change in timing of the cash receipt of up to four months makes the consequences of a customer switching highly significant to cash management.

Cost recognition

Cost is recognised on the income statement in exactly the same way as revenue. A cost is incurred when the benefit of products or services is received. The benefit may not necessarily arise at the moment the items physically arrive in a business: for example, manufacturing components will go straight into inventory until they are required. On the income statement there is a principle of "matching" whereby the costs of providing products and services to customers are matched with the income derived from their sale. Hence the benefit of components used in producing products arises at the point of sale not the point of manufacture.

Regardless of whether components are used immediately or are held as inventory, they are likely to be paid for 30–90 days after they have been delivered. Costs incurred but not yet paid for are the payables or creditors on the balance sheet, representing supplier accounts waiting to be settled.

As well as the liability of payables there is the liability of accruals. Accruals are an estimate of the cost of products or services where the benefit has been received, or partly received, and for which an invoice has not yet formalised the amount owed: for example, electricity consumption that is invoiced in arrears once a meter has been read. An accrual is therefore an estimated payable that is used as a way of ensuring that all costs are correctly included in reporting profitability. Accruals are likely to be settled after payables, but both are imminent cash outflows.

Interpreting an income statement

An income statement represents activity done and not cash movements. It reflects how profitable or not a business is, but not the business's cash position. The timing effect of the various events in a manufacturing business is shown in Figure 1.2.

In many businesses the only financial information that is given to operational managers is an income-statement style budget report. With no information on the cash flow, these managers have little incentive or ability to monitor or manage it.

Asset values

The balance-sheet item that usually consumes the most amount of cash is fixed assets, which includes land, buildings, machines and vehicles. It follows that fixed assets may also have the potential for raising the most cash should it be required. However, the amount shown on the balance sheet will not reflect the current market value of the fixed assets. Instead it will be based on the following principles:

■ **Historical cost.** Assets are recorded at their original cost less any depreciation (see below). Where an asset may have increased in value it is not usual (though it is possible) to revalue it upwards. This is partly because of the fickle nature of the market, but more importantly the value is only indicative until a transaction is concluded. This is particularly relevant for bespoke assets for which there may be either a limited or no resale market.

FIG 1.2 **Timing effect of events in a manufacturing business**

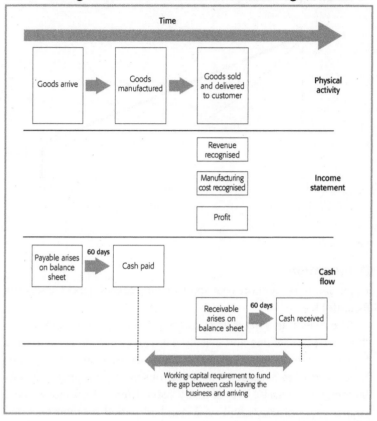

■ **Impairment review.** The directors are required to review the portfolio of assets each year and assess whether there is any permanent diminution of value or impairment in any of them. Write-downs should then be made to adjust for any overstatement.

The effect of these principles, if they have been prudently applied, is that in the case of assets such as buildings, where market prices may have appreciated, there can be latent value that is not evident from the balance sheet.

FIG 1.3 **Straight-line depreciation**

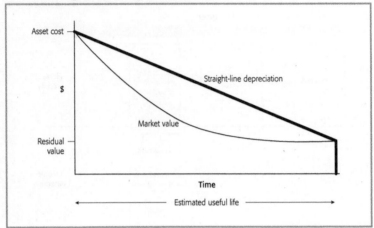

Depreciation

Depreciation is the process of spreading the cost of a fixed asset over its useful life.

The cost of an asset is its purchase price and, where appropriate, the costs of delivering and installing it. The useful life of an asset is based on management judgment. Some assets, such as computers, have short lives because of technical obsolescence; others, such as buildings, have useful lives of many years. Therefore businesses pool similar types of assets and set a standard period for their expected useful life: for example, for freehold buildings it might be 50 years, whereas for computers or cars it might be only three or four.

Several methods can be used to spread the cost of owning an asset. Most businesses use straight-line depreciation, which effectively spreads the cost evenly over an asset's useful life.

If an asset is to be scrapped at the end of its useful life, the cost of ownership is the purchase cost. Should an asset, such as a motor vehicle, be disposed of before its value reaches zero, the total amount of depreciation to be spread over its useful life will be its cost less any potential residual value.

Figure 1.3 shows that straight-line depreciation will result in a potentially higher than market value being shown on the balance sheet for assets, such as computers, whose market values can drop fast after purchase.

Making sense of balance-sheet assets

Where a business is trading successfully with good cash flow the mismatch between the market value of fixed assets and the value shown on the balance sheet is unlikely to be a problem. These assets are being held for their use not their market value, and the mismatch will disappear over time and be inconsequential. Only when an asset is no longer needed or there is a cash crisis that requires it to be sold would its market value become relevant. The management of assets is covered in Chapter 5.

In contrast to fixed assets, many of the other assets on the balance sheet are shown at values that are a reasonable indication of their actual value. Management is responsible for regularly reviewing inventory to write off surplus or unsaleable stock and receivables to write off bad debts. Inevitably, the judgments management make on what to write off may be wrong – more or less stock may prove unsaleable or some bad debts may turn good and be paid.

Provisions

The main operating liabilities are payables and provisions. Payables, as stated above, consist of specific short-term liabilities that are usually settled within a few weeks. Provisions are future obligations that are uncertain in both amount and timing. The amount of a provision is based on the concept of prudence, which requires that all liabilities and potential liabilities should be included on the balance sheet or disclosed. Conversely, the concept requires that revenues and profits should only be included once their realisation is reasonably certain.

Examples of provisions include the funding of a shortfall in a company pension fund, potential warranty responsibilities for a manufacturing business, or commitments to restore sites after mining activities are completed. Provisions will only become payables once a liability is formalised by one or more future events. For as long as they remain provisions rather than payables, there is not normally a need to have cash immediately available to meet them.

Making sense of balance-sheet liabilities

Although a balance sheet differentiates between short-term (less than a year) and long-term (more than a year) liabilities, the difference is of little help in identifying how much cash is needed to meet imminent liabilities, let alone what is due to be paid and when in the longer term.

To really understand a business's cash payment obligations, a cash flow forecast is required, providing details of what cash receipts are expected to come in and when, and what cash payments are required or expected to go out and when. From this detail, likely shortfalls or surpluses of cash can be identified and action taken to make sure there are funds in place to cover shortfalls or make productive use of any surpluses. The development of a cash flow forecast is covered in the next chapter.

2 Cash flow forecasting

A BUSINESS HAS A RESPONSIBILITY to make payments when they are due regardless of whether sufficient cash has been collected from customers to provide the means of payment. Unpaid suppliers may be begrudgingly tolerant and wait a little longer for their cash, but they may refuse to fulfil further orders until payment is made and they may even take legal action to recover the debt.

To enable management to plan appropriately and feel confident that payments can be made as they fall due, a detailed cash flow forecast is required that predicts the timing and amounts of receipts and payments. The advance warning of any potential cash shortages that are revealed allows management the time to put together a considered, rather than reactive, plan for bridging any gaps in cash flow. It can take time to negotiate with banks and raise additional finance, and with a well-structured and realistic cash flow forecast this can be done well in advance of any potential need.

Furthermore, a well-constructed cash flow forecast helps give banks and other providers of finance confidence in management realism and competence – and can encourage banks to lend at less onerous interest rates than they otherwise might.

This chapter looks at the construction of the most important tool in managing cash and avoiding a cash crisis – a cash flow forecast. It explains how this links to the business plan and how to manage anticipated cash surpluses or deficits.

Cash flow forecasting

The essence of constructing a cash flow forecast is to take the current cash balance and predict the likely receipts and payments that will arise within a set of time intervals. The quality of the predictions determines the quality of the cash flow forecast and its usefulness. What the cash flow forecast is to be used for – funding, operational or strategic purposes – will determine the time period and time intervals:

■ For operational planning a much more detailed near-term forecast is required. This might be daily for the week ahead, weekly for the next two months and monthly for a further 12 months.

■ For negotiations with banks a common approach might be to make monthly predictions for either two or three years with annual totals.

■ For strategic planning an overview forecast is generated that will be quarterly or annual for up to ten years.

When cash flow is strong a simple monthly forecast may provide sufficient operational control, but for many businesses, and in particular if cash becomes tight, a weekly or even daily cash flow forecast is required. This level of detail is necessary because of potential mismatches that can take place within a month. For example, a large outflow in the first week of a month could be offset by a large inflow in the last week. In aggregate there would appear to be no problem, but for the middle two weeks a significant cash deficit may need to be carried. Provision is required to manage all deficits, however long they may last.

All forecasts need to be reproduced at least monthly (even weekly or daily in the case of some operational forecasts), with omissions or variations in one forecast being carried over to the next, such as the delay in purchasing an asset. An actively managed cash flow forecast will provide far more useful information than a historically prepared outlook. Cash flow forecasts are like newspapers: they are only of use on the day they are written.

In its basic form, the forecast begins with the current month and the current cash balance. The likely receipts and payments are then added and subtracted. The resulting cash balance for one month then provides the opening balance for the subsequent month and so on.

TABLE 2.1 **A cash flow forecast, $'000**

	Month 1	Month 2	Month 3	Month 4	Month 5
Opening balance	6,000	5,200	6.400	(1,500)	(2,000)
Receipts	8,300	(12,600)	4,900	8,800	11,600
Payments	(9,100)	(11,400)	(12,800)	(9,300)	(9,200)
Closing balance	5,200	6,400	(1,500)	(2,000)	400

Table 2.1 shows that there is a mismatch in receipts and payments that creates a deficit in months 3 and 4. These need to be covered by one or more of the following:

- a cash investment;
- the use of an overdraft facility (a temporary loan);
- the deferral of purchases or payments that fall due in months 3 and 4 (such as the acquisition of assets);
- the acceleration of receipts that arrive in month 5 (perhaps by offering discounts for early settlement).

These options will be explored in greater detail later in the book as each one may provide a quick cash flow solution, but in the longer term may undermine the operation of the business. For example, a delay in the purchase of an asset will defer the revenue from the products or services using that asset; similarly, a discount for prompt settlement from a customer sets a precedent that may undermine longer-term customer profitability, and so on.

Business unit and consolidated cash flows

For larger businesses that comprise a number of business units or subsidiary or group companies, a cash flow may be generated for each business. Rather than planning to deal with the surpluses and deficits that arise in each, surpluses in one unit can usually be used to offset deficits in another and vice versa. Therefore for cash flow management the overall group cash position is what will ultimately need managing and funding. The cash flow forecast process should require each business unit to generate their own cash flows; these are then summarised (or consolidated) into one overall cash flow that removes all inter-business-unit transfers.

In some group structures, where there are subsidiaries or business units based in different countries or currencies, this is not a simple process. Complications include the costs of foreign-currency conversion and the realisation of exchange gains or losses through translation from one currency to another, as well as interest identification issues that require each legal entity to be able to declare its interest income and cost for tax purposes. Multi-currency and multi-country businesses are covered in Chapter 3. For the purposes of cash flow forecasting, each currency should be consolidated and treated separately.

A detailed cash flow forecast

While a simple forecast may predict the likely cash surpluses and deficits in the business each month, it needs to be much more specific in the analysis of the sources of receipts and destination of payments to make it informative to management and a practical planning schedule. It should be structured in five categories:

- Operating items – sales receipts, costs and wages
- Non-operating items – taxation and loan interest
- Capital items – assets and investments
- Equity dividends – distribution of profits
- Funding items – shares and loans

With a structured cash flow the business performance can be more easily assessed. For viable trading the net cash flow from the operating items should be positive. If the core activities cannot regularly generate a cash surplus, there is unlikely to be a long-term future for the business.

Ideally, the cash from operating activities should be sufficient to meet the non-operating commitments of taxation and interest and still leave a surplus that can contribute towards the replacement and expansion of the asset base.

The cash flows for capital items can be split into two types:

- Stay in business (SIB) capital – the money spent on the replacement and renewal of assets that are already in use in the business. This spending is almost unavoidable; for example, a software business generally needs to replace workstations and servers every few years to keep pace with technology changes.
- Expansionary capital – the money spent on incremental assets to expand operations (resulting in the creation of new revenue streams or saving of operating costs). This spending may be discretionary and therefore if cash is constrained the purchase can be postponed without necessarily affecting existing operations.

Once SIB capital expenditure is deducted from the net operating and non-operating items, effectively all payments necessary to maintain the current business activities have been made. A subtotal can be drawn at this stage, which is known as free cash flow. Ideally, this amount should be positive so there is a choice over its use: it could be invested in expansionary capital for the business, distributed to investors (by way of a dividend or share buy-back), or used to repay investors' financing. The repayment option is explored further in Chapter 7.

If free cash flow is negative, this will be the minimum amount that needs to be externally funded to keep the business trading at its current levels. The structure of a cash flow forecast is illustrated in Figure 2.1.

Debt expressed as a multiple of free cash flow is often used by banks to determine default risk and may well form one of the lending covenants. Thus careful monitoring of this subtotal, and achieving certain ratio values to satisfy investors, can have a significant influence on the way a business is managed and determines the pace of growth.

An expanding business is unlikely to be able to generate enough of its own cash to fund the two types of capital investment. In particular,

FIG 2.1 **Structure of a cash flow forecast**

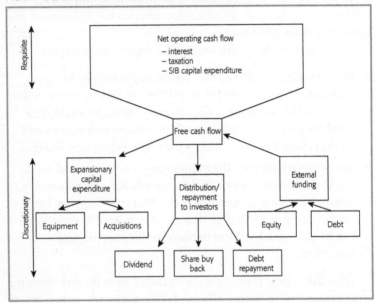

the expansionary assets acquired will help in the generation of future cash flows and therefore external finance is likely to be needed up front to enable their purchase.

Lastly, any equity dividends to be paid are shown and once all the future receipts and payments are identified, the net cash position can be calculated. This will form the basis of the funding decisions. Sources of finance will need to be selected to cover deficits and receive surpluses. The various funding options are explained in Chapter 3.

Table 2.2 illustrates a more detailed and structured cash flow.

In putting together a detailed cash flow forecast, many of the numbers can be drawn from the business plan or budget to which it should be aligned. The process used in producing a budget will identify future expected sales volumes, revenue, operating costs and capital investment. However, a budget is based on identifying monthly activity levels and profitability at the time the service or product is delivered, but the cash flow effect usually has a timing offset for the date of settlement. For example, in a budget a business

TABLE 2.2 **A detailed cash flow forecast, $'000**

	Month 1	Month 2	Month 3	Month 4	Month 5
Opening balance	1,000	200	280	60	50
Operating items					
Cash sales	4,800	3,200	4,100	4,400	4,300
Cash from credit customers	7,300	7,200	7,800	6,100	6,700
Wages & salaries	(2,900)	(2,900)	(2,900)	(2,900)	(2,900)
Payments to suppliers	(5,200)	(5,100)	(5,100)	(5,100)	(5,200)
Distribution	(380)	(400)	(400)	(390)	(410)
Overheads	(1,200)	(1,200)	(1,200)	(1,200)	(1,200)
Marketing	(600)	(100)	(900)	(300)	(200)
Cash flow from operations	1,820	700	1,400	610	1,090
Non-operating items					
Sales tax (net)	(900)	0	0	(1,000)	0
Income or corporation tax	0	0	0	0	0
Interest expense	(120)	(120)	(120)	(120)	(120)
Cash flow before capex	800	580	1,280	(510)	970
Capital items					
SIB capex	(1,600)	0	(700)	0	0
Free cash flow	(800)	580	580	(510)	970
Expansionary capex	0	0	(2,100)	0	0
Other asset additions and disposals	0	0	300	0	0
Cash flow before dividends	(800)	580	(1,220)	(510)	970
Dividends	0	0	0	0	0
Cash balance before financing	200	780	(940)	(450)	1,020
Financing items					
Loan drawdown	0	0	1,000	500	0
Loan repayment	0	(500)	0	0	(1,000)
Share issue	0	0	0	0	0
Closing balance	200	280	60	50	20

might plan to produce 5,000 units in July and sell them at $10 each. The revenue invoiced and shown in the budget for July would be $50,000. But the customers may take 1–3 months to pay, which will spread the cash receipts over the period August–October and perhaps even beyond for a few late payers. Understanding this mismatch in the timing of events is critical in cash planning as the staff costs to produce, sell and distribute these units are likely to be paid in advance of the receipts. The cash needed to fund the timing difference between paying out for products and services and receiving payment from customers is known as working capital, which is explained in more detail in Chapter 4.

Techniques to build each area of a detailed cash flow forecast are described below.

Operating items
Receipts

Cash from the sale of products and services arises in two ways: cash sales where the receipt is at the point of sale, and credit sales where receipt can be a month or more after submitting an invoice for the products or services supplied. To forecast these receipts you need to know three things:

■ unit volume of products and services sold;
■ prices of products and services sold (including any discounts);
■ credit terms and the typical profile of customer receipts (including any bad debts).

Forecasting unit volume of sales

Unit volume of sales is probably the most difficult part of the cash flow forecast to predict. It is almost entirely based on external factors and involves the greatest number of unknowns (such as economic conditions, customer behaviour and competitor activity). All the other areas of the cash flow forecast are either a factor of the unit volume of sales (such as unit costs) or a discretionary amount (such as marketing). Hence deriving a reasonably accurate forecast for unit umes is central to creating a credible cash flow forecast.

The forecasting process is the same as that used for activities such as strategic planning, business planning and budgeting. Four broad techniques can be used:

■ **Market analysis.** Market size, market segments, competitor activity, market share, product life cycles and price points are all taken into consideration by marketers to gauge the market for a business's products and services. The process should quantify the market growth (or contraction) expectations over the forecast period. Identifying potential market growth will provide a context for how the business can be developed. Understanding the competitive environment will help evaluate the opportunity for or threat to growth in market share. With a defined market and market share an indicative forecast unit volume can be derived. For more on the process of market analysis see *The Economist Guide to Business Planning* by Graham Friend and Stefan Zehle.

■ **Projections.** An arithmetic extrapolation of past data and trends, the assumption being that past performance will predict future performance. Experience shows that this is rarely the case as economic conditions and competitor activity inevitably change the pattern of sales volume. There can be some merit in this type of projection for a small business, such as a restaurant, where a simple table occupancy rate can be calculated based on past experience. Regression and moving averages are the mathematical techniques most commonly applied in this type of forecasting.

■ **Correlation.** An arithmetic determination of volume based on the forecast of externally derived indicators. Alignment to indicators or a combination of indicators such as GDP, average incomes and employment or unemployment rates would be common. A correlating formula is generated that is based on fitting the external data to past performance. A mathematical model can then use the independently produced projections of these external factors to derive the future sales volume. As with projection, a numerical relationship may not maintain its validity in the future.

■ **Judgment.** Someone who has been in an industry for many years, seen competitors come and go, seen boom and recession, seen customer loyalty and disloyalty, and so on, will have sufficient experience to be able to offer a reasonably credible short-term forecast. Although this technique may produce remarkably accurate results, it is difficult to use it in funding applications as there is little evidence to support the conclusions drawn. However, where a business has only a few customers an open discussion with the larger ones may elicit some indicators of future commitment. With such data and an element of judgment an indicative level of volume increases or decreases from past levels can be predicted.

Whichever technique is used, it should be validated by one or more of the others. If projections using all four methods give similar results, this is likely to generate far more confidence than one method on its own. The danger in using any of these techniques is that it is too easy for results that "do not fit with our expectations" to be dismissed rather than investigated further. Where senior management demand to see growth, forecasts showing growth are what they will be presented with regardless of whether the compiler of the data genuinely believes the numbers that have been prepared. It is only in an environment of honest debate that realistic data will emerge and allow appropriate responses to any shortcomings that are identified.

Where a cash flow forecast is being regularly updated the historic projections can be compared with what actually happened and the forecasting techniques that were applied can be refined accordingly. This will support future projections and increase confidence in them. There will always be errors in any projection caused by unexpected external events, so the aim is to reduce the size or narrow the range of likely errors rather than to attempt to eliminate them.

Although these forecasting techniques use the same processes that might be used for generating a sales budget, any assumption made at budget time should be reviewed to see if it still holds true. Often budgets are the result of an annual process that takes place up to six months before the start of a financial year. Nine months or a year later and in a volatile market their continued relevance can be questionable. Some businesses use rolling forecasts instead of annual budgets; aligning cash flow projections to this process would avoid duplication of effort and ensure a congruence of management information.

With an indicative forecast unit volume derived from these techniques, the tactics required to "farm" the existing customer base and "hunt" new customers can be created. The necessary activities to support these customer retention and marketing plans can then be included when compiling the cost side of the cash flow forecast.

Care should be taken to ensure that the sales volume forecasts fairly reflect seasonal factors. This can be done most easily using previous years' data, allocating 100% to a full year's sales and then calculating the proportion of 100% that occurs in each month or week. An even distribution will therefore have 8.33% of annual sales occurring each month, but most businesses, perhaps with the exception of basic foods, are unlikely to have an even profile. It is important to identify the months when sales will be low as this can lead to a cash strain. For example, if a business is likely to have a poor August because its usual customers are on holiday, then in October, or whichever month the bulk of August's sales invoices are paid, there will be a low level of cash receipts. Adjustment should also be made for events such as Easter or Ramadan, which can fall in different months each year, or particular weather conditions that can cause spikes or troughs in sales. Hence the overall sales volume pattern may have consistency with previous years, but will need appropriate adjustments to ensure it reflects the expectations in each of the months ahead.

Forecasting prices of products or services

The prices to use in the first few periods of the cash flow are likely to be those currently being charged for the existing portfolio of products and services. Thereafter pricing will be intrinsically linked to the sales volume forecasts defined above, because of the typical relationship between price and customer demand. If prices are increased, this is likely to reduce demand, and vice versa. A typical price–demand curve is shown in Figure 2.2.

Understanding the sensitivity of a product or service to changes in price is crucial for optimising revenue and cash receipts. This

FIG 2.2 **A typical price-demand curve**

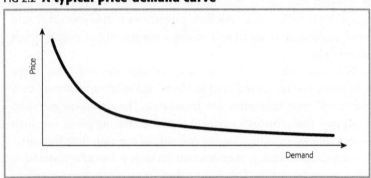

sensitivity is known as the price elasticity of demand and depends on, for example, competition, substitutes, how much the buyer needs the product or service and the scale of the purchase in proportion to the buyer's income.

For a highly inelastic product or service, such as the latest type of mobile-phone handset, a price increase may be the most effective way to generate more cash as price is not the most important criterion in buyers' minds and thus an increase will have a minimal effect on overall demand. For a highly elastic product or service, such as gasoline, a price reduction may be more effective as this could generate substantial extra demand. The price reduction strategy (permanent or temporary) would be particularly opportune where a business has significant spare capacity or a high level of inventory.

In setting the prices to use for the cash flow forecast, it is important to include the appropriate levels of any discounts that may be offered, such as:

■ customer or trade terms – pre-negotiated discounts for customer loyalty;

■ bulk purchases – discounts based on order quantity;

■ overriders – an annual discount based on achieving defined volume targets;

■ settlement – prompt payment (the value of offering this type of discount is covered in Chapter 4);

■ promotions or sales – a discount to all customers for a short period of time.

In some businesses the "list price" is rarely achieved as it is seen as the starting price from which a discount is deducted. In such situations what matters is the final price paid. The psychology of selling suggests that an inflated price with a big discount is more appealing to customers than a lower price with no discount – even if the net amount paid is the same.

Most businesses price products and services in the currency of the country in which they trade. Where there are sales in other currencies, a business will need to manage its exposure to any movement in exchange rates and the cost of conversion back to the main trading currency. For occasional small transactions it is unlikely to be worth investing time in managing this risk. For a business such as a travel company, whose business is based on sales in one currency and costs in another, this is a crucial issue. Managing foreign-exchange risk is covered in Chapter 3.

Credit terms and payment profile

For a business with credit sales the length of credit taken by customers can be identified from an analysis of past payment history. Based on this a realistic estimate can be made of when the cash will arrive, and of the proportion of bad debts. The payment profile might be, for example:

■ under 30 days – 11%
■ between 30 and 60 days – 45%
■ between 60 and 90 days – 28%
■ between 90 and 120 days – 14%
■ bad debts – 2%

Using such a payment profile the sales conversion into cash can be calculated. Normally, the cash flow forecast is drawn up on a calendar-month basis, and while some customers might pay their invoices on the last day of one month, their cash may not arrive in the bank account until the first or second day of the subsequent month. In such situations it is appropriate to record receipts in the month they arrive, otherwise there may be insufficient cash in the bank at the end of the month. As a lot of payments may go out at the end of the month, clarity on the precise timing can be significant at this point in the cycle.

With the payment profile shown above, the cash received in any month is the addition of the relevant proportion of the sales made in the current and each of the previous three months. Table 2.3 shows how the sales made in each month are collected.

TABLE 2.3 **Sales per month, $**

	Sales	Cash in month 1	Cash in month 2	Cash in month 3	Cash in month 4	Cash in month 5	Cash in month 6
Month 10	91,000	12,740					
Month 11	87,000	24,360	12,180				
Month 12	93,000	41,850	26,040	13,020			
Month 1	68,000	7,480	30,600	19,040	9,520		
Month 2	79,000		8,690	35,550	22,120	11,060	
Month 3	84,000			9,240	37,800	23,520	11,760
Month 4	95,000				10,450	42,750	26,600
Month 5	102,000					11,220	45,900
Month 6	109,000						11,990
		86,430	77,510	76,850	79,890	88,550	96,250

The total cash collected in month 4 is $79,890, which is 14% of the sales in month 1, plus 28% of the sales in month 2, plus 45% of the sales in month 3, plus 11% of the sales in the current month.

It is also assumed that 2% will never pay. While this is effectively excluded every month, the impact is likely to be more dramatic when it actually occurs. The first sign of a customer in trouble is the slowing of receipts; then receipts cease; then a bad debt is declared. The exposure may well be for several months' worth of sales. The importance of managing credit limits and monitoring late payment is critical to ensure that the signals are detected early, accounts are stopped (to prevent further goods or services being supplied) and potential bad debts are minimised. The principles of managing receivables are covered in more detail in Chapter 4.

Payments

Payments cover direct costs (the costs incurred to provide the products and services) and indirect costs (the costs of managing the business). In forecasting the cash flow for operating payments, there are four considerations for each item:

- Fixed or variable – is the cost dependent on or independent of volume?
- Frequency – how often is the payment made?
- Price – the cost of the purchase made.
- Credit terms – the timing of the payment after the receipt of products or services.

Before looking at these in detail, perhaps the most important aspect of the payments part of the cash flow forecast is completeness of the cost categories. Any costs that are omitted will make the cash flow look healthier than it should and lead to potential underfunding. Cross-referencing the cost category list to the business's accounting system, purchase orders and business plans for new projects will improve completeness. However, it is common for some sundry categories to be combined in one rounded amount with an element of contingency rather than listed individually by how they are recorded in the accounting system.

In projecting a cost the first consideration is how the cost behaves in relation to unit volume of sales. There are two typical behaviours: fixed and variable.

Fixed costs

Fixed costs are those that, in the short term, stay constant as changes in unit volume of sales occur. An example is rent paid for premises. A small increase in business activity is likely to be able to be accommodated within the existing premises and hence the cost will

FIG 2.3 **A fixed cost**

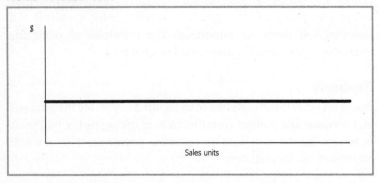

not rise as volume rises. It is important to note that the "fixed" aspect relates only to volume of activity and not to price. The cost may still be subject to the impact of inflation and periodic rent reviews. Figure 2.3 is a graph of a fixed cost.

If this graph shows the annual rental of a delivery vehicle, for example, it will be valid for the delivery of any number of sales units up to the vehicle's capacity. However, if sales volume continues to rise the business will need an additional vehicle, and the graph will become stepped (see Figure 2.4).

The most difficult point at which to operate is just before the step rises. In this example, the vehicle would be working at maximum capacity to meet demand. Pressure to deliver may compromise

FIG 2.4 **The effect of an additional fixed cost**

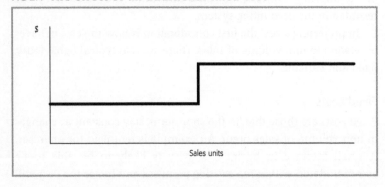

FIG 2.5 **A variable cost**

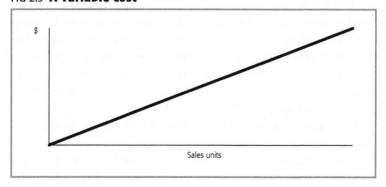

planned maintenance of the vehicle and, in the desire to make the maximum use of it, cause suboptimal prioritisation of customer fulfilment. Once a second vehicle is brought in there will be plenty of idle capacity across the two vehicles but twice the rental payment. Although this provides a good opportunity to improve customer service, profitability will decline until volume increases and both vehicles are appropriately utilised.

A crude operational optimum for many such fixed costs will be 75–85% utilisation of available capacity. This allows for the handling of uneven work patterns and the operation of a proper maintenance schedule.

FIG 2.6 **The effect of volume discounts**

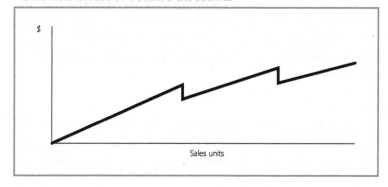

Variable costs

Variable costs are costs that increase as volume increases or decrease as volume decreases, sometimes referred to as incremental costs. An example is components used in manufacturing: the more products that are made the greater is the volume of components required. Figure 2.5 is a graph of a variable cost for low volumes, reflecting a linear relationship.

As volumes increase there is likely to be greater purchasing leverage with the supplier, so volume discounts can be negotiated. The volume discounts cause the cost to rise more slowly, which brings down the unit cost. This is essential to understanding the third item in forecasting payments: price. Figure 2.6 is a graph showing this effect.

An example would be $1 for the first 2,000 units, 80 cents per unit for quantities up to 4,000 units and 60 cents per unit for more than 4,000 units.

Semi-fixed and semi-variable costs

Many costs are a combination of fixed and variable elements. An example is salaries, which are typically fixed, but overtime and bonus payments are usually variable. Similarly, electricity can be a mixture of the two. In a manufacturing environment the electricity for lighting and heating a factory is fixed, but the electricity to run the machines is variable. In such cases, if the cost is small in relation to the overall cost base, it is normally categorised by its predominant nature.

Having established whether each cost is fixed or variable, the unit volume for the variable costs can be linked with the projected sales volume identified in the revenue section of the cash flow forecast. There may need to be an allowance for waste, as putting 100 units into a process will not always result in 100 units coming out. Damage, faults and theft will cause losses requiring some additional purchases to be made.

Frequency

A regular monthly pattern of payments is much easier to predict and manage than large, irregular payments that create an uneven demand for cash. For example, property rent is typically paid quarterly, so a business must plan to ensure there is sufficient cash to meet this obligation when it falls due.

The frequency of payments needs to be understood and built into a cash flow forecast. Each payment has a frequency of one of three types:

- Monthly – occurs every month, for example monthly wages and salaries.

- Intermittent – happens regularly but not monthly, for example rent or utilities that may be quarterly.

- Occasional – happens infrequently (annually or as required) such as insurance or legal fees.

The three types of frequency are listed in order of ease to forecast. Monthly payments may well be constant payments that can be forecast with reasonable certainty. The most difficult to predict are occasional payments, such as legal costs (where services are used as they are required), a bad debt, an employment dispute or a contract negotiation. In such cases it would be reasonable to look back at past frequency of activity, perhaps once or twice a year, and put in an allowance for such payments evenly distributed through the year. In this way a cash provision builds up so that the funds are available should they be required.

Price

Short-term prices for each cost can be based on existing arrangements with suppliers, but longer-term prices are likely to rise (though potentially some may also fall). Therefore the extrapolation of price to future periods can be made using one of the following:

- Contract rates – where a contract exists that may set prices for a period or the mechanism by which they will inflate for subsequent periods, for example property rent.
- Indexation – linkage to external or government indices that provide indicative rates for expected price rises.

If indexation is to be used, it is unlikely that one index will be suitable for all payment categories. Examples of indexes are as follows:

- Consumer price index (CPI). This is a government index designed to represent the average inflation for a basket of goods and services that an average family might purchase. In the absence of another index, this would be the best to use in calculating annual inflation in costs.

- Payroll. For many years, in developed economies, payroll inflation rose faster than goods and services inflation. This was partly a result of operational efficiency, but also because cheaper imported goods, particularly from Asia, replaced more expensive locally produced goods. Inflation may not be the only factor affecting forecast payroll prices; others include employer tax changes, staff promotions and even increases in pension fund contributions to cover deficits.

- Energy. As global demand for energy has increased the prices of oil and gas have risen. The 2008 banking collapse reduced global demand and prices fell, but as economic activity increases so will energy prices. For industries such as airlines, steel and pottery energy is a substantial part of the cost base, so price volatility is a major consideration. The cost of energy can rise fast yet sales prices may be agreed in advance and take time to be realigned. Thus there may be a profit and cash squeeze until margins can be restored.

- Industry specific. Some industries have their own inflation factors. In telecommunications, for example, there has been deflation for many years as technology improvements have reduced the cost of providing capacity and bandwidth. The effect of this on many businesses would be insignificant in comparison to their overall cost base, so a separate index would be appropriate only for businesses with a significant proportion of their payments in this area.

Discounts

Prices for purchases should be net of trade and volume-based discounts. It is not necessarily optimal for a business to accept a prompt-payment discount, as this will accelerate payments out of the business in return for a percentage reduction. The decision should be based on comparing the settlement reduction with the cost of debt.

Would the business be better off repaying debt for a month or taking the discount? A simple comparison of interest rates should help in making the choice. The interest rate to use is normally the overdraft rate, as any temporary cash shortage caused by accelerated payments will incur overdraft interest.

In making the comparison it is important to have the interest rates in the same terms. For example, a 1% prompt-payment discount for paying a month early cannot be easily compared with a 10% annual overdraft rate.

Converting an annual interest rate into a monthly interest rate is more complicated than simply dividing by 12. The compound interest effect must be taken into account, so the following formula is required:

$$\sqrt[12]{(1 + 10\%)} - 1 = 0.7974\%$$

This shows that a 1% prompt-payment discount provides better value despite the potential overdraft interest of just under 0.8%.

Purchases from abroad may be denominated in a different currency from the one used to prepare the cash flow forecast. When projecting payments into the future, price inflation and exchange-rate volatility should be considered. If a business makes significant purchases abroad, it can be helpful to hedge the currency risk and lock into a predetermined rate. Although this will remove any exchange-rate gains, it will also exclude any exchange-rate losses; and if product or service margins are narrow, then certainty on costs can ensure the products or services stay viable. The process of hedging is covered in Chapter 3.

Credit terms

The credit terms taken on payments are much the same as those explained above for receipts. When purchasing products or services, it is common to take a period of credit before payment. As the settlement of accounts payable is under management's control, there is a temptation to push them out as far as possible, though there are implications for a business's relationship with suppliers and its overall image – it may make suppliers less willing to supply or less conscientious, or it may encourage them to increase their prices to cover the cost of the credit provided.

A business trying to defer payment is at odds with a supplier trying to reduce its receivables. What is needed is a contractual agreement that is accepted by both parties and complied with for all payments. Without such an agreement with key suppliers, the actions taken by each party will undoubtedly lead to strained relationships as each pushes its preferred position.

It is common for the agreed settlement date to be at the end of the month following the month of invoice. Therefore any products or services purchased in, say, March will be paid for at the end of April. In the cash flow forecast, payment will be made in the month after the product or service has been received.

Non-operating items

This category involves payments for non-trading items that have to be paid on specific due dates with possibly serious consequences if settlement is delayed. It includes most taxes, such as sales taxes, income tax or corporation tax, as well as interest payments on financing. Less important but also included are any investment receipts such as interest or dividends.

Taxes

Tax payments are likely to be calculated from the forecast trading activities. Sales taxes can be based on total sales or be a net payment to the government (that is, tax charged on sales minus tax incurred on purchases). The calculation of the amount owing is based on the "tax point" for all invoices sent and received, which is usually the invoice date. It is therefore possible that tax will have to be paid on sales before the cash has been received from the customer. There are schemes to help small businesses avoid this effect, but larger businesses may have to fund the timing difference themselves.

Income or corporation tax is levied on profits. There are various allowances and deductions before a percentage rate is applied. The rules for this calculation are both extensive and complex, and are specific to each country or jurisdiction. There are also exemptions available for particular business classifications and activities. It is important to remember that a cash flow forecast is based on estimates, so an indicative tax number is required rather than a detailed calculation. A common approach is to review past years and use similar percentage rates, taking into account any changes made by the government. The tax may be paid in arrears, biannually, or in quarterly instalments. If payment is in arrears, a business has a strong cash flow advantage because some of the profit being taxed may have been earned at least a year in advance of the payment.

It is common for cash payments for payroll taxes to be included within the operating items, so the cash flow for wages and salaries is the total payment, not just the payment made to employees. This simplification ignores the fact that payroll taxes may be paid in the month after the employee is paid, and thus the benefit of this deferral is lost. If the amounts are significant, there should be separate lines in the cash flow for the employee part and the government part of the payroll cost.

Interest

Interest costs arise on debt instruments at varying rates and payment points. Most debt instruments also have fees that have to be paid at the outset and on renewal of facilities.

Fixed-rate loans for a fixed term are the simplest to forecast. For variable-rate loans the uncertainty is in predicting the interest rate that will prevail. One way to determine market expectations for interest rates is to look at the yield curves quoted in the financial media. These show the market rates for future-dated bonds relative to the current base rate. This indicates what the market expects to see happening to interest rates in the future.

The most difficult cost to model is interest being earned on a current account or paid on an overdraft. These temporary balances are difficult to predict and can be wildly inaccurate. A common way of dealing with this is to take the average of the opening and closing balance for each month (or forecast period), and then either earn or pay the interest that arises. If this calculation is being done in a spreadsheet, it may well cause a circular argument error. (This is because tax is paid on the profits and the profits are calculated after interest, yet the interest is calculated on the cash balance, which is the total after paying the tax.) One way to overcome this problem is to assume that any interest on the current account (providing the amount is small) is excluded from any tax calculation. Another method is to use a tax-adjusted interest rate such that a net interest rate is used.

Capital items

As explained above, capital expenditure is usually split into two types: stay in business (SIB) and expansionary. For both types there is a cash flow impact at purchase and again at disposal.

SIB capital expenditure

A useful guide to the amount of SIB capital expenditure required is the reinvestment ratio, which compares the annual depreciation charged to annual SIB capital expenditure as follows:

$$\frac{\text{SIB capital expenditure}}{\text{Depreciation}} \times 100$$

If the ratio is less than 100% (investment is less than the depreciation of assets), a business may be milking its assets and moving towards an unsustainable state where either the assets will require higher maintenance or a significant amount of new investment will be needed. This is a criticism levelled at governments that minimise investment in areas such as transport infrastructure.

In normal circumstances the ratio should be more than 100%, as the effect of inflation will make the replacement cost of assets higher than their depreciating historic cost. If the measure is substantially more than 100%, a business is investing more than its assets depreciate and therefore the selling price of products and services should be increasing to make the investments justifiable and maintain profitability.

Expansionary capital expenditure

The amount of expansionary capital expenditure is normally set at budget time and a number of projects have to bid for their share of a limited resource. The development and structure of a business case for a new project is explained in Chapter 5.

The difficulty in forecasting the capital expenditure cash flow relating to new projects is that the actual projects may not have been identified at the time the forecast is prepared. Therefore a crude assumption will be that the total capital budget will be spent evenly over a year.

The pace of growth in a business can be dictated by its ability to raise funds to purchase infrastructure. In such circumstances, an outright purchase may not be the most appropriate way to gain access to an asset. In Chapter 5 the advantages and disadvantages of renting, leasing, franchising and outsourcing are explained. These are methods of gaining access to assets without the need for large amounts of initial finance, but there are conditions, contracts and costs that may make the access less flexible or more expensive than an outright purchase.

Other asset additions and disposals

Many other types of capital assets are bought and sold, including:

- Investments – long-term investments in other businesses, primarily through the purchase of shares, including strategic stakes, joint ventures or whole businesses.
- Intangibles – brands, patents, rights, trademarks, copyrights and other intellectual property.
- Biological assets – plants and plantations.
- Software – off-the-shelf products and bespoke systems.

Cash flow from capital items

For asset acquisitions, the amount includes the purchase price as well as any costs in getting the asset to its location and condition of use. Thus the cash flow forecast will show the total cash outflow required to obtain the asset. If the purchase is spread over a period of time – perhaps a deposit on placing an order or stage payments during construction – the timing of payments is significant. They should be placed in the correct month in the cash flow forecast.

For a disposal, any cash received may involve a period of credit being taken by the purchaser. In some cases, a disposal may involve a payment for the asset to be removed, decontaminated or recycled.

It is important to note that there is no mention of depreciation appearing as a line in the cash flow forecast. This is because depreciation is a way of spreading the cost of an asset through to the income statement during the period of use (see Chapter 1). In a cash flow forecast only cash transactions are shown, so depreciation or amortisation has no place in it. With assets transactions take place on purchase or disposal and usually nothing in-between.

Forecasts for asset purchases are usually aligned with business plans, but it is common for capital expenditure to become delayed. However, performance targets may require project managers to demonstrate that the project is under way by the end of the financial year. This can result in a rush of payments being made in the closing months of the financial year that plays havoc with the false sense of liquidity the delay had engendered. The way to avoid this is through good and open communication between project managers and the finance function.

Dividends

A business's dividend policy may be explicitly stated, or investors may infer it from the dividend payments it has made in the past. The policy usually involves a target pay-out ratio (the proportion of earnings that will be distributed). Being able to deliver on the dividend policy is a critical part of managing investor expectations and attracting equity into a business. However, cash that is paid out of the business cannot be used for reinvestment or to provide security for additional borrowings. Therefore a dividend is a reduction in equity that can curtail growth and reduce the potential for value creation.

To some extent dividends signal management confidence in the cash generation of the company, and will:

■ increase when management expect that the business can continue to pay higher dividends long into the future, a state of affairs that can increase share price;

■ decrease when a business is facing financial difficulty with the consequence that its shares are less appealing to investors and the price falls.

Although the dividend payments are shown in the cash flow

forecast alongside other discretionary uses of cash, the reality is that once a dividend stream is being paid to investors there are negative consequences to its level being reduced. Businesses maintain their dividend for as long as possible, even with declining performance, and may defer capital investment in order to preserve it.

The payments of cash to investors may be annual, biannual or quarterly. Typically, the interim dividends are smaller than the final dividend as they are declared on forecast results. Only when the financial year has ended can the final results be known and the appropriate dividend declared. The final dividend will therefore be paid perhaps 4–6 months after the end of a financial year.

Financing items

One of the main reasons for producing a cash flow forecast is to identify the future funding surpluses or deficits. Knowing the monthly balance enables management to determine any requirements for increases or decreases in debt and equity. The negotiation with investors and securing of finance can take place ahead of its need and thus ensure business continuity.

The first stage in this section of the cash flow forecast is to enter any capital repayments on debt, bonds and some types of convertible and preference shares that are required under the terms of their original financing. This does not include interest payments as they are shown in the non-operating part of the cash flow forecast. It is important to identify any refinancing requirements as the business, the economy and interest rates may have substantially changed since the original finance was secured. The terms for new finance could be quite different and significantly change the profile of investment in the business such as a move from longer to shorter terms or syndicated rather than single sourced debt.

With all the cash flow items included the resulting balances on the cash flow forecast may well have some peaks and troughs, but this does not necessarily mean that a large overdraft facility should be used to manage the troughs. Overdraft is normally the most expensive form of debt finance and should be used only for temporary mismatches in cash flow. More importantly, banks like to see an overdraft cleared to zero at least annually otherwise it is effectively a loan.

FIG 2.7 **Funding requirement for a three-year period**

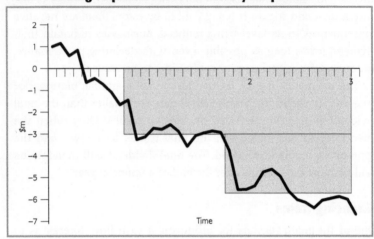

To identify appropriate funding, the final cash flow profile of balances should be taken and funding strips mapped on top that can be the basis of specific loan or equity funding. Funding strips are medium-term blocks of capital that last at least a year and are of sufficient size to make the fund-raising worthwhile. Fees are likely to be involved in raising debt and thus it can be uneconomic to raise small amounts.

In the example in Figure 2.7, a three-year cash flow forecast shows that two separate $3m loans will be needed to fund the majority of the deficit. One loan will start in month 9 and the other in month 21. The remaining gaps can be filled by overdraft, by drawing down the loans early or by deferring some capital expenditure. The funding gap in months 7 and 8, where there is a temporary deficit of over $1m, is the main concern.

The same profile after including the two loans is shown in Figure 2.8, with cash surpluses and deficits now being contained within a balance of plus or minus $1m.

Once new finance is identified the necessary interest payments should be included in the non-operating part of the cash flow. This will of course affect tax payments and the final surplus or deficit.

This is an example of a simple loan transaction. The full range

FIG 2.8 **Revised forecast with loans included**

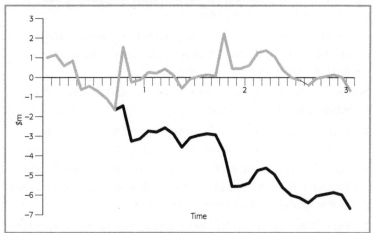

of funding options, techniques to manage the net balance and the security of an overdraft buffer are covered in Chapter 3.

Contingency

The aim of a cash flow forecast is to provide realistic information on which sound planning can be based. However, forecasts are based on estimates and assumptions and are therefore inexact, so an understanding of the level of uncertainty and the range of results that can be accepted is necessary. It is more important to explore the types of results that will trigger changes in management actions (and their probability of occurring) than to pursue spurious accuracy.

Before considering an amount for contingency it is worth looking at the culture of the organisation that has prepared and will be using the forecast. Some of the problems that distort the forecasting process are as follows:

■ Management find it difficult to cope with unexpected results – they need someone to blame if it goes wrong and thus contributors use external references and avoid using their own judgment.

- Protracted debate about the right forecast – arguments about who has the more valid view of the world.
- People are "punished" for getting the forecast wrong – there are delusions of accuracy and an unwillingness to accept that unlikely events can indeed happen.
- Pressure to provide detail – a search for confidence in a process where detail does not exist.
- Year-end focus – an inability to see beyond the end of the financial year and the achievement of key indicators at all costs.
- Disorganisation – parts of the business can have better insight into what is happening in the market, but they are not consulted as this would create a sense of deference.
- Distortion – bearers of bad news prefer to avoid the consequence and thus give the forecast management wants to hear even though the originator may know it to be wrong.

Any of the above make it likely that some of the cash flow forecasts will already have an element of contingency built into them. What should be avoided is building in contingency at each level and then again for the whole business. The most appropriate method is to make each line as realistic as possible and have just one line of contingency at the end that can be flexed to explore sensitivity to changes in market expectations and assumptions.

Inevitably there will be areas, such as new projects, where there is great uncertainty about the amount and timing of particular payments. In this case it is best to include them at their earliest possible point of payment and thus enable the appropriate financing to be planned. It is also worth highlighting and annotating these items so that those using the forecast can consult project managers for up-to-date information before specific financing decisions are made.

The main issue in forecasting is not the degree of error in assumptions and estimates, but the failure to identify the need to make an intervention as a consequence of the forecast result. It is far easier to convince yourself that a forecast is wrong and needs to be made "more in line with our thinking" and thus justify "no action is required" than to have the courage to take significant actions that are revealed by unexpected results.

For a more detailed understanding of how to address these issues and forecast successfully see *Future Ready* by Steve Morlidge and Steve Player.

Cash flow measures

In reviewing and judging the quality of a business's cash flow, several measures are commonly used. Many have been explained above, but they can be summarised as follows:

- On the detailed cash flow forecast shown in Figure 2.2, the cash from operations should be positive as should free cash flow. These subtotals indicate that the core operations are generating sufficient cash to cover the costs of being in business. Positive free cash flow is the more important of the two as it is after tax, interest and SIB capital expenditure.

- To measure whether the debt investors are at risk, it is important not only to generate sufficient cash to be able to pay the interest, but also to limit borrowings to what can be ultimately repaid.

- To judge interest serviceability, the cash from operations is divided by the total interest cost. This gives a multiple of how many times the interest could have been paid. A minimum of three is normally required.

- To monitor the borrowing capacity (explained further in Chapter 3), the total debt should be no more than a multiple of six times EBITDA (earnings before interest, tax, depreciation and amortisation).

- For shareholders, the measure of cash flow per share can be a useful indicator of performance at both the operating cash flow and free cash flow levels.

Financial reporting style

This chapter has focused on producing a cash flow forecast, which is not the same as a statement of cash flows used in a set of published reports and accounts and produced in compliance with International

TABLE 2.4 **Cash from operations**

US	UK	Amount	Explanation
Operating income	Operating profit	25	The operating income from the income statement
Add back depreciation and other non-cash deductions	Add back depreciation and other non-cash deductions	10	In arriving at operating income several items have been deducted that do not involve cash leaving the business, including depreciation and provisions. Hence these need to be added back
Movement in inventory	Movement in stock	3	The money tied up in funding an increase in inventory (or released on a reduction in inventory)
Movement in receivables	Movement in debtors	(5)	The money tied up in funding an increase in receivables (or released on a reduction in receivables)
Movement in payables	Movement in creditors	(3)	The money made available by increasing payables (or spent by reducing payables) amount
Cash from operations	Cash from operations	30	The cash generated from trading

Accounting Standard (IAS) 7. The main differences are as follows:

■ The cash flow forecast is produced to help plan what the business will be doing in the future; the published statement is normally used to report what has been done in the past.

■ The forecast is based on estimates and assumptions about the future; the published statement is based on history and the actual transactions that have taken place.

■ The forecast is in a free format and constructed to help make management and financing decisions; IAS 7 prescribes the layout allowed for a published statement.

The reporting format of the operating activities can also be different when the IAS 7 "indirect method" is used; the published statement will build on the income statement (where most of the operating items already appear) and avoid duplication by starting the

TABLE 2.5 **Condensed cash flow statement**

US	UK	Amount	Explanation
Cash from operations	Cash from operations	30	As calculated above
Tax paid	Tax paid	(5)	Tax paid to a government, which typically lags behind the cost shown in the income statement. This is because the full cost cannot be worked out until the profits have been calculated
Investing activities	Investing activities	(40)	Cash spent on buying (or received on selling) new fixed assets or acquisitions. Also including any interest received and dividends on investments
Financing activities	Financing activities	30	Cash raised on drawing down of further loans or issuing of additional share capital (or from repaying either of these sources of finance). Also includes any interest and dividends paid to investors
Change in cash in the business	Change in cash in the business	5	Surplus cash available for the following year

published statement of cash flows with the line of operating income. However, operating income is not the same as cash from operations so a series of adjustments are made for non-cash items in the income statement and any movements in working capital. With this method, the line "cash from operations" can be reached in only five lines of data (see Table 2.4).

The operating income is the earnings before interest and tax, but in calculating this figure items such as depreciation and amortisation have been deducted. Therefore these need to be added back to derive the earnings before interest tax, depreciation and amortisation (EBITDA).

EBITDA is a good approximation of the cash generated by the business from trading; it is not exact because the revenue and costs are recognised on the income statement when the products or services are delivered rather than when the cash is received or paid (see Chapter 1). Therefore to calculate the cash from operations the movement in the opening and closing working capital items needs to be included.

For example, in the current year the business should receive the cash from the receivables held at the beginning of the year, but not from the receivables held at the end of the year. Hence the total cash received in the year can be expressed as:

Cash received in year = opening receivables + annual sales − closing receivables

Similar adjustments are made for movements in inventory and payables.

The remaining cash flow statement is much the same as the one shown earlier in this chapter though condensed down into fewer sections and losing the subtlety of the two types of capital investment and the line of free cash flow (see Table 2.5).

3 Treasury management

A DISTINCTION IS OFTEN MADE between cash management and treasury management. The difference may be subtle with the former being more operational and short term and the latter being more strategic and long term. Essentially, treasury management is an extension of cash management in both time horizon and sophistication of activities. The typical ranges of topics that are covered by each are shown in Table 3.1.

TABLE 3.1 **Cash management or treasury management?**

Cash management	Treasury management
■ Banking operations	■ Cash-management policies
■ Collections and payments	■ Financing strategy
■ Liquidity monitoring and short-term cash flow forecasts	■ Long-term cash flow forecasts
■ Working capital management	■ Relationships with credit agencies and financial institutions
	■ Financing of deficits
	■ Utilisation of cash surpluses
	■ Hedging interest rate and foreign-exchange rate risks

Many of the cash-management principles are covered in other chapters. The focus of this chapter is on banking operations, liquidity monitoring and the financing aspects of treasury management.

Banking operations

For banks, the most lucrative area of operations has been investment banking, which primarily helps businesses raise capital, trade securities and derivatives, and manage mergers and acquisitions. An expansion of investment-banking activities and a weakening of controls were to a large extent the cause of the global financial crisis. Regulation is intended to tighten the scope back to the traditional role, and the precise nature and profitability of these activities will emerge.

The branch networks provide business banking, which covers transaction services through current accounts, borrowing and deposits. The day-to-day services are usually far less profitable, but they are crucial for building a customer base that will, from time to time, require investment banking services.

To attract business customers, the banks set out to offer a range of services at attractive costs or even "free". At the centre of their offering is usually a relationship manager whose job it is to acquire new customers, retain existing ones and maximise the customer lifetime value (through each customer buying its products and services). Electronic banking will be offered including free software that strengthens dependence and will help to increase the adhesiveness of the customer to the bank. Over time the relationship manager should get to know a business, know its key staff, offer timely advice and introduce appropriate banking services to the business. The relationship manager is the access point to all the bank's services and should therefore play an important role when it comes to a business wanting to raise funds, a temporary overdraft or credit references.

It is important that business customers balance the bank's advice with independent advice and thus make sure the bank identifies the right products at the right price. Customers should be prepared to change banks to secure the portfolio of services that offers them the best value for money.

Table 3.2 illustrates some of the main services offered by most banks (or a subset offered by other financial institutions such as credit unions and commercial banks). The first thing to focus upon in selecting a bank is its willingness to lend. Finding a bank that will offer funds with the rate and flexibility to match the needs of the business is paramount. Most of the other services are usually available with little differentiation, particularly in transaction services.

TABLE 3.2 **Principal banking services**

Transaction services	Receipts and payments (electronic, paper, cards, cash and foreign)
	Statements
	Pooling and sweeping arrangements
	Letters of credit/guarantees
Savings and investment	Call and deposit accounts
	Money market investment
	Securities and other tradable investments
Borrowing	Overdraft
	Loans
	Commercial mortgages
	Invoice factoring
	Leasing/hire purchase
Investment banking	Debt raising (syndicates and bonds)
	Equity raising: public and private placing (IPO and rights issues)
	Asset finance (secured on receivables, inventory, or property)
	Mergers and acquisitions
	Securitisations
	Risk management and derivatives
Additional financial services	Insurance: property, business, key man and health
	Debtor insurance
	Pensions

Transaction services

The current account will handle all a business's receipts and payments so every transaction will pass through this account at some stage. In structuring transaction services there are several aspects to consider.

Cost of running an account

There are five types of transaction that are likely to pass through the current account:

- Physical cash (deposits and withdrawals).
- Paper (lodgements and cheques) – this type of transaction is diminishing as a means of settlement and countries such as the UK have considered phasing out cheques altogether.
- Electronic (receipts and payments) – the most common way for one business to transact with another.
- Card (credit and debit card receipts and payments) – the most common way for a business to transact with an individual consumer.
- Foreign (exchanges to or from a business's trading currency).

The cost of running a current account normally consists of a monthly account maintenance charge and transaction charges that depend on type, with electronic transactions being cheaper than others.

Security

In a world of sophisticated fraud, businesses need strict internal controls over account access, payment originations, authorisations, validations and reviews. These internal controls need to be operated in conjunction with a bank to ensure there is rigorous application. And they need to be set as much, if not more, to prevent internal fraud by staff rather than external fraud. Internal safeguards should also protect innocent staff from false suspicion or accusations of wrongdoing.

The controls can be made easier to operate by using multiple bank accounts with transfers between them. For example, a set of accounts might be as follows:

- A receipts account for receiving payments from customers. The account number is printed on every invoice and statement and thus becomes widely distributed. However, no withdrawals are allowed from this account except through authorised transfer to another of the business's accounts, thus preventing fraudulent withdrawals.
- A low-value payments account for amounts under, say, $10,000 or $25,000 to be drawn to pay for everyday supplies. The

payments are bulk generated by the accounting system and may have lower authorisation requirements than the high-value payments account. If operated in conjunction with the bank, large payments are stopped and duplicate payments to the same account can also be stopped, thus reducing high-value fraud.

■ A high-value account for amounts over the limit set for the low-value account to be drawn. There should be strict authorisation controls that are structured so that it is – in theory – impossible for anyone to act alone in making payments from the account.

■ A header or sweep account where surpluses and deficits from all the other accounts are pooled at the end of each day so that the overall surplus or deficit can be managed efficiently (see below).

Cash pooling and sweeping

As explained above there are good reasons to have more than one business bank account. There may be benefits in having a larger set of bank accounts, extending the list above to include one for each branch, office or subsidiary, one for each currency where there are regular transactions, and so on.

Once the number of accounts increases there is the potential to lose out on the interest spread, with some accounts in surplus earning low, if any, interest and some in deficit paying high interest. Moreover, a business does not want to be constantly making transfers between accounts to net off the surpluses and deficits. Far better for all the accounts to be pooled so that there is one overall surplus or deficit that can then be managed efficiently to maximise interest earnings or minimise interest costs.

There are many banking products that can assist with either automated physical daily transfers or notional transfers to create a pooled arrangement. The various strategies available are shown in Table 3.3.

Banks have a set of charges for each of these options covering both service and transaction fees. The cost versus benefit of each option must be assessed in selecting the most suitable method to optimise the cash in the business.

The pooling process can be done across an entire business, though

TABLE 3.3 **Bank account transfer strategies**

Basic	No pooling	All accounts are left with individual surpluses and deficits. Interest is earned or charged on each account accordingly
	Manual pooling	The business originates manual transfers to move money between accounts including foreign-exchange transactions to convert cash residing in foreign-currency accounts. Interest is earned or charged on each account accordingly
	Automated zero or trigger balance transfers	Each night the bank automatically sets every account to zero by pushing or pulling the net balance to or from a header account. Foreign-currency accounts are only swept when their balance is over a trigger level to avoid the costs of small transactions. Interest is based on the single header-account balance
	Single-currency notional pooling	Each night the bank automatically generates a mirror account that notionally pulls balances to one account while leaving the physical cash surpluses and deficits in their original accounts. Interest is paid or charged based on the single notional balance
Advanced	Multi-currency notional pooling	The same process as for single-currency notional pooling except foreign-currency balances are also notionally mirrored in the single account by using the current exchange rate to convert them into the base currency

this can create tax complications if there are separate legal entities in the group. Each separate legal entity needs to be able to report its own interest income and expense. Therefore the notional pooling option is more appropriate, with the interest rate on the group's overall net balance being used as the basis to charge or earn interest on each of the individual accounts.

The more sophisticated notional pooling arrangements are not offered in most of Africa, South America and parts of Asia. This is where using a global bank can be advantageous as it can organise automated physical transfers for some parts of the business and notional for the rest.

Statements

To monitor liquidity and the validity of the payments that have been made, it is important to see bank statements at least daily if not in real time. Therefore access to online facilities needs to be established and procedures set up for completing regular bank reconciliations.

Bank reconciliations are used to compare and match the cash movements in the accounting records with those shown on the bank statements. Differences can be caused by items in the process of being presented or cleared, unrecorded items in the accounting records, discrepancies and errors. All differences need to be checked to ensure that nothing unexpected has occurred.

Letters of credit and guarantees

These are forms of assured payment between a supplier in one country and a customer in another. They are explained in more detail in Chapter 4.

Savings and investments

Fundamentally, a product- or service-based business should not be trying to build a substantial cash surplus. As explained in Chapter 1, the aim of a business is to produce a sustainable return on investment that is greater than that of a savings account. Excess cash should be reinvested or returned to investors on the principle that it should be "earning or returning". There will be day-to-day surpluses and at times a need to build some cash reserves before events such as a major investment, debt repayment or dividend payment. The business should have a policy on the amount of cash to hold (known as the target balance); this is explained later in this chapter.

Any surpluses that are held need to be invested in order to generate income. However, the highest returns are normally achieved by either locking the cash away for a specified term or putting it into higher-risk investments, neither of which are consistent with the business purpose. Therefore in deciding where the surplus should be invested the objectives of low risk and access must be paramount.

Call and deposit facilities

Each day there will be a net balance on the individual, pooled or swept bank accounts. When there is a surplus, a bank can be instructed to automatically place the money on deposit overnight to earn interest and then have it paid back the following morning. This is operationally efficient though not necessarily financially efficient as overnight deposit rates tend to be low. A higher rate can be obtained from a longer-term deposit. There are three commonly available types of account:

■ Call account – money can be withdrawn instantly.

■ Notice account – notice is required before a withdrawal can be made, for example 7, 14 or 30 days.

■ Term deposit – money is deposited for a fixed period and usually at a fixed rate of interest.

The maturity dates of a deposit should be matched to the cash flow forecast of operational needs. Thus it would be rare for a business to need a 90-day notice option as within that time frame there may be opportunities for debt repayment or new investment, both of which would be expected to provide a better rate of return than these deposit accounts.

Money market

Money market deposits are short-term instruments, typically with a maturity of under 13 months (capital markets offer longer-term instruments). For example:

■ Certificates of deposit. Promissory notes issued by a bank with a fixed maturity date and interest rate. As banks are highly regulated this type of deposit should be classed as low risk, but this is questionable following the banking collapses of 2008, making a spread of risk across several banks a safer option.

■ Commercial paper. A short-term promissory note issued by a business, but with a fixed maturity of less than 270 days, usually issued to finance their receivables or inventory. This will be the highest risk of this category of savings, though it is possible that some businesses issuing commercial paper may have a better credit rating than some banks.

■ Treasury bill. Short-term debt obligations issued by the American government that mature within 3–12 months. They are usually auctioned so the discount on the maturity value provides the equivalent of interest. Government debt is usually regarded as the safest form of deposit, though this too has become questionable in the aftermath of the banking bail-outs and country credit-rating downgrades.

Generally, the weaker the credit rating of the institution issuing the instrument the higher is the rate of interest offered. Interest rates that are substantially higher than those available in deposit accounts can be easily achieved, but there is the risk that a weaker institution may default.

Securities and tradable investments

The capital market provides longer-term options through bonds, equities and longer-dated government securities. As noted above, a trading business will have little need for investment in these areas, but these are the types of products used by pension and savings funds for the majority of the cash they manage.

Borrowing

There is a range of borrowing types as shown in Table 3.4. In selecting the most appropriate type of debt finance for a business there are two main determinants: duration and cost.

Duration

How long is funding required? The duration of funding will have a significant influence on which type would be most suitable. In principle, the repayment of funding should match the profile of the investment it is used to finance, thus long-term assets should be funded by long-term finance and short-term assets by short-term finance. For example, property and plant might be funded by debt or equity instruments as they are both long-term investments. However, an increase in receivables or inventory as a consequence of seasonal business activity might be funded by an overdraft as the cash investment is likely to be repaid in a few months.

Cost

What is the cost of funding? There are two types of cost: the initial set-up fees and the interest on the money for the period it is borrowed.

TABLE 3.4 **Types of bank borrowing**

Type	Duration	Cost	Risk of repayment	Purpose
Overdraft	Normally has a fixed time period	A facility fee as well as a variable interest rate significantly higher than central bank rate	Depends on security arrangements but can rank behind other forms of debt	To bridge day-to-day working capital gaps between receivables and payables
Loan	Often fixed-term with a predetermined repayment date and sometimes interim repayments, though they can be 'evergreen' where they are routinely renewed leaving the principal remaining outstanding for the long term	An arrangement fee as well as a percentage return that can be fixed or variable. The variable rate is usually linked to a central bank rate plus an increment	Ranks before all shareholders and will sometimes be secured with a fixed or floating charge on assets	Funding for projects that will generate sufficient funds to allow repayment
Commercial mortgage	Usually a fixed-term loan that is secured on freehold property	Similar to a loan though the nature of the security means it will normally carry a substantially lower interest rate than an unsecured loan	Ranks before all shareholders and will be secured with a charge over a building	Long-term funding for premises

Type	Duration	Cost	Risk of repayment	Purpose
Invoice factoring	The outsourcing of debt collection and hence the duration of the debt is for life of the contract (see Chapter 4)	A management fee as well as a discount on the debts being factored to take account of the interest cost on the money advanced to cover the time taken to collect the debt	Secured on the debts. Factoring can be done with recourse (any bad debts passed back to the business) or without recourse (the lender accepts liability for any bad debts, but the bank will charge a higher fee for this)	To accelerate the collection of receivables and prevent cash being tied up in working capital. It can also be used to reduce overhead costs as it outsources part of the accounting function
Leasing	For the life of the asset being leased (see Chapter 5)	Normally a fixed interest-rate cost implicit in the monthly payments	Secured on the asset being leased	To obtain the use of assets without an upfront purchase. There can also be potential tax and replacement benefits

Set-up fees are charged for a range of services such as arranging a facility or line of credit, making a commitment, renewing a facility, taking a legal charge over assets and the non-drawdown of a facility. Each of these fees is typically between 0.5% and 1.5% of the amount borrowed. Therefore the annual cost of debt may carry an interest rate of, say, 8%, yet with fees this can easily exceed 10%.

The interest paid on the money borrowed depends on the risk taken by the provider of the funding: the higher the risk the higher is the rate of return they require. For example, if a provider of funds is promised that it will be the first to be repaid if the business gets into difficulty and that it can take a charge over the physical assets (such as property that it could sell to clear the debt), it has a low risk of losing its money and thus the business would expect the cost of this funding to be low. However, lowering the risk to one provider of funds increases the risk to another. If all the assets are used as security for one party, another will have no security that its money will be repaid in the event of difficulty. For this higher risk a higher return will be required. The cost of funding is therefore determined by the level of risk associated with each type of funding.

In summary, the cost of funding is determined by risk, both absolute to the business activities and relative to the risk position of other investors.

This section on borrowing covers smaller-scale and shorter-term funding options that are typically sourced from a single bank or financial institution. More sophisticated types of fund raising are considered in the later section on investment banking.

An important consideration with any of these types of borrowing is that the lending criteria may be suitable at the time the transaction is initiated, but will it still be the right choice should the business grow or contract? Inflexibility and in particular penalty clauses have caused many businesses to regret commitments they had undertaken. For example, a business decides to obtain a property on a five-year lease rather than borrow money and buy it. If the space becomes too big or small for its requirements, it can be expensive to exit the lease. In such a situation a business may end up moving to new premises and trying to sublet its old building. Negotiating flexibility and exit options may prove a valuable investment of time and legal costs at the time the transaction is initiated.

For small or start-up businesses the existing assets base and financial track record may provide insufficient security for funds to be lent. In such cases personal guarantees from the founders and directors may be required as security. Should the venture fail, the bank will call upon the guarantee and seek repayment from the sale of personal assets such as the family home. Avoiding the need for personal guarantees should be a high priority in selecting both the type of finance and the amount drawn down.

Investment banking

Investment banking services are used by businesses that wish to raise capital from the markets, either equity through a share placing or debt through a bond issue as shown in Table 3.5. The fees for these services can be high and thus appropriate only for raising significant amounts in excess of, say, $5m. These fees may have three components:

- An upfront or monthly retainer for consultancy services, of which the main one is to help develop a business plan to justify the amount of capital being raised and to provide evidence to investors that the business is viable and participation is worthwhile.

- A fee paid upon completion of a transaction, sometimes referred to as a "success" fee. The fee will amount to between 2% and 10% of the total capital raised, with equity being two or three times as expensive as debt – typically 5–10% for equity and 2–4% for debt. (The difference in percentages creates a strong incentive for investment banks to recommend clients raise equity rather than debt.) For this fee the bank will create a prospectus, agree financing terms (called "term sheets"), solicit investors, negotiate proposals and help the company complete the transaction.

- Equity compensation in the form of warrants. The warrants usually have an exercise price equal to the issue price of the equity sold. They provide an incentive to investment banks to make the equity issue successful (though may encourage them to underprice a transaction so that they gain on the increase in stock price).

Investment banks are also involved in other market-based transactions:

- Asset finance. Raising various forms of debt for long- and short-term purposes to fund assets such as inventory.

- Mergers and acquisitions. Advising on transactions to acquire another company as well as defending a company from being acquired.

TABLE 3.5 **Types of investment banking services**

Type	Duration	Cost	Risk of repayment to investor	Purpose
Syndicated loan	Similar to the loans described in the previous section (see Table 3.4). However, if the loan is too large for one bank (too much risk in one counterparty) it will share it with others, forming a syndicate that is managed by a lead bank	An arrangement fee as well as a percentage return that can be fixed or variable. The variable rate is usually linked to a central bank rate plus an increment	Ranks before all shareholders and will sometimes be secured with a fixed or floating charge on assets	Funding for projects which will generate sufficient funds to allow repayment
Bond	Fixed with a predetermined repayment date	Fixed interest-rate return. Varieties of straight, deep-discount and zero-coupon. Interest may be paid during the life of the bond, at the end or a mixture of the two	The loan is issued in certificate form that can be traded like shares. Bondholders are paid out before all shareholders	Long-term loan finance with a cash flow profile to match the cash profile of a project in which the funding is invested

Type	Duration	Cost	Risk of repayment to investor	Purpose
Ordinary shares or common stock	Permanent finance raised as an IPO when first taken to the market or at a subsequent issue (rights issue). Once shares are issued they are not normally repaid, though there are legal processes available to allow a share buy-back	Usually through dividends paid out of earnings	Ordinary shares are tradable securities though their liquidity depends on the market. Leading stocks are easily realisable but stocks in small private companies can be difficult to trade. Ordinary shareholders are the last to be paid in event of a winding up so these investors have the highest risk of losing their money	Ordinary shareholders own the company and provide the core long-term funding. The equity also provides security for debt providers
Convertibles	Permanent capital first as debt then as equity. There can be a repayment option if the share price at conversion is not attractive	A low interest-rate return for a set period, followed by conversion into ordinary shares providing the share price has achieved a specified level	Although a form of debt, convertibles usually rank after other debt. Once converted to ordinary shares, the risk is the same as the other shares	Long-term finance that has a low initial cost

■ Securitisation. The selling off of a portfolio of assets to a special purpose company (SPC) in which investors buy shares. The SPC receives income from the underlying assets and may have recourse to the original business in the event of default. This is an effective way to convert assets, such as a portfolio of customer receivables, back into cash. However, it became a widely used technique in the credit boom where smaller banks would load their balance sheet with domestic mortgages, parcel them up into an SPC, and then turn them back into cash with a securitisation. The cash was then used to grant further mortgages. This all worked well until some of the mortgages started to default and the credit risk reverted to the original bank. Investors found banks had accumulated combined exposures in their SPCs that were far greater than banking regulation would allow if they had kept all the mortgages on their own balance sheets. The catastrophic effect of high default rates saw the demise and subsequent rescue of many banks around the world.

Additional services

Additional services are also available as part of a business banking relationship, though these have limited involvement with cash management and thus are covered briefly.

Insurance

There are several types of insurance available for a business, covering obligations to the public, customers and staff. A business can also get insurance to protect investors from losing assets through fire or theft, to protect revenue through professional or product indemnity and other contingencies.

Pensions

Many banks will also be interested in helping to provide a business with pensions for its employees either through its own pension management business or through brokering a scheme with an independent management company.

Liquidity monitoring

Chapter 2 covered the development of a short- and medium-term cash flow forecast to predict the profile of cash surpluses and deficits for up to three years. Liquidity monitoring is more concerned with the short-term part of this forecast: today, this week and up to three months ahead. The aim is to forecast the bank balance that will result at the end of each day, allowing management to plan how to cover deficits and make best use of surpluses, thus maintaining cash availability to the business.

The liquidity template has similar elements to the basic cash flow template illustrated in Chapter 2; all that is required is to know the list of receipts and payments. It can be helpful to separate the cash that is formally committed or advised from the cash that is expected. This is the difference between hard (committed) and soft (expected) numbers.

The forecast starts with a bank reconciliation to establish the opening balance after all the latent transactions in the system have cleared. The main differences are likely to be cheques that have been sent to suppliers but not yet been presented for payment. An example is shown in Table 3.6.

TABLE 3.6 **Bank reconciliation**

	$'000
Bank balance today	1,800
+ Lodgements presented but not yet credited	200
− Payments (cheques) made but not yet presented	(640)
Balance available after all existing transactions have been processed	1,360

The daily projections are shown in Table 3.7.

As with all forecasts these are estimates and of course subject to change, although most of a one-week forecast can be made with a reasonably high level of accuracy. The payments are invoices that have been processed in the accounting system and are due for payment on particular dates. It is the receipts that are uncertain; customers

TABLE 3.7 **Daily projections, $'000**

	Day 1	Day 2	Day 3	Day 4	Day 5
Balance at start of day	1,360	2,140	2,140	2,573	2,583
Receipts					
Customer advised	780	0	0	410	0
Expected	0	0	1,233	0	90
Payments committed					
Suppliers	0	0	0	0	(2,564)
Payroll	0	0	0	0	(1,400)
Rent	0	0	(800)	0	0
Payments expected					
Asset instalment	0	0	0	(400)	0
Balance at close of day	**2,140**	**2,140**	**2,573**	**2,583**	**(1,381)**

may send advice notes indicating that a cash receipt is imminent, or receipts can be estimated from contract terms. For cash sales, a typical day (seasonally adjusted) could be used as an expected value.

The receipts could be developed further with a schedule showing each customer, the invoices issued and the likely date of collection. However, to avoid the schedule becoming overlong, it can help to limit it to bigger customers, with small items (making up no more than 10–20% of the balance) combined and listed as one item. After several months a pattern of payment behaviours for each customer will emerge making future forecasts increasingly accurate.

With the profile of closing balances now available, a plan for covering the deficits and investing the surpluses can be made. The separation of the committed and expected items allows a more robust plan to be made. In the example above, even if the expected receipt on day three does not materialise, the account will still be in surplus. It is only on day five that a deficit arises of a likely $1,381; but if none of the expected receipts arrive, this could be as much as $2,704.

The policies required to deal with covering any deficits and optimising any surpluses are explained below. They need to cover both the short and the long term as the actions will be different.

Therefore as the amounts involved grow, it is important to make sure that longer-term procedures are in place to raise additional finance or utilise surpluses.

In monitoring liquidity it may be necessary to differentiate between cleared and uncleared funds. This applies only to paper-based receipts as electronic transactions are of cleared funds. A business may not be able to draw upon money from a cheque paid into the bank for 3–5 days, even though it may appear on the bank statement. In the bank clearing system the money needs to be withdrawn from the cheque issuer's account and transferred to the presenter's account with validation of authenticity along the way.

Cash-management policies

To operate the cash balances in line with long-term strategy (to which they may not be privy), finance and treasury managers need a set of policies (or guidelines) that define how surpluses and deficits should be treated. Such polices should be prescribed for each of four eventualities:

- cover for short-term cash deficits;
- investment for short-term cash surpluses;
- sources to draw down long-term finance;
- application for long-term cash surpluses.

The overriding aim of the policies is to ensure uninterrupted business operations with cash available as it is required. The second is that the business should be funded at the lowest cost without carrying large inefficient surpluses.

Cash profile

The first stage of policy setting is to decide whether the business will normally run with a cash surplus, a cash deficit or an equal frequency of each. To determine this, the daily cash balance profile can be plotted using the forecast values (as derived above).

Figure 3.1 shows a normal distribution graph that may not be exactly the profile revealed but is likely to have similar characteristics with a predominance of values around one amount and some extremes.

FIG 3.1 **A normal distribution**

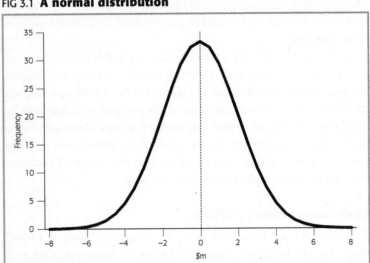

The next question is where to set the central point (or target value). In Figure 3.1 it is zero with a few points at the extremes that are +/−$6m from the centre. This is an illustration of a business that aims to run with a target of zero cash and surpluses and deficit arise with equal frequency.

As overdraft interest rates are one of the most expensive forms of finance, it may be more cost effective to draw down a larger loan and have the central point or target balance set at, say, $2m. Thus the range of balances in the example would be from −$4m to +$8m and lead to an average holding of $2m at any point. Using normal standard deviation calculations this would mean that a deficit would arise on only around 17% (or 60 days a year).

It would be unwise for a business to push this target value much higher as there would be a significant amount of cash sitting on deposit for much of the year, and with the interest rate spread this would be an expensive buffer. Conversely, banks would not want to see the balance constantly in deficit. By its nature an overdraft is meant to be temporary and thus it should be cleared at least once a year; otherwise it is effectively long-term finance for which a loan would be cheaper.

Before deciding on the average balance, a business should consider whether it needs an operating or temporary cash surplus. There may be several reasons for this:

- To absorb setbacks. Smaller businesses operating in sectors such as house-building that have an unpredictable profile of receipts and struggle to raise loans from banks may need a "just in case" reserve.

- To manage the peaks and troughs of a cyclical business. Capital-intensive firms have a much harder time maintaining cash reserves as they have both infrastructure and inventory to carry with long lead times. For example, car manufacturers, steelmakers and airlines have to ride out cyclical downturns when cash flow dries up.

- To cover short-term fluctuations. Troughs in cash flow cycle are likely to occur in businesses where receipts are seasonal, project-based or come from only a few large customers.

- To plan for growth. Preparing for an asset purchase or an acquisition rather than repaying debt, only to draw it back down again soon after. This would be done only in the short term, perhaps 3–6 months before the purchase.

- To finance a specific project. Providing start-up funds for a new activity where there is uncertainty about the timing and ability for it to generate its own cash flow in the short term.

An example of an amount of cash to hold as a reserve would be sufficient to pay for X weeks of expenditure. Determining X depends on the reliability and frequency of receipts. For example, if a business receives most of its receipts at the end of the month, X might be four. If the business is a retailer with daily cash receipts, X might be a week, and so on.

Cover for short-term cash deficits

Based on this analysis, the business shown in Figure 3.1 would set its policy at holding around $2m as its target cash balance and take an overdraft facility for up to $3m. This would still leave a few instances a year (perhaps no more than three or four) where the business might need an overdraft of more than this. With plenty of warning, identified through liquidity monitoring, it may be possible to defer some expenditure by a few days to avoid exceeding the limit, or indeed to get the bank to agree to a temporary excess. This excess can be negotiated with clear expectations of when it will be back within the limit.

Investment for short-term cash surpluses

All surpluses should earn interest at the highest rate possible, without putting the money at risk. Paying down an overdraft is nearly always the best use of cash, though prepaying other forms of debt may not be possible without incurring substantial penalties. In the absence of an overdraft, short-term deposits will provide an income. With reliable liquidity monitoring it may be possible to achieve better deposit rates by using fixed-term or notice accounts – seven- and sometimes 14-day fixed deposits are commonly used. If the rates for these investments are substantially better than a simple deposit account, it may be worth using them even if an overdraft is required for one or two days during that period. Understanding the interest-rate spread is critical to optimisation.

It is unlikely that the surplus will be sitting in one fixed-term deposit. Having it broken down into several separate rolling deposits starting and finishing on different days means that cash is regularly becoming available rather than all of it being locked away.

Sources to draw down long-term finance

When the need for an overdraft becomes persistent and the cash flow forecast indicates that the situation will not improve for at least three months, longer-term finance of either debt or equity should be considered as it will be cheaper than an overdraft. This depends on the required duration of the finance and the accumulated risk position of the pool of investors as explained later in this chapter.

Application for long-term cash surpluses

When there is an accumulation of a cash surplus that is forecast to remain for at least three months, a business has three options:

- Investment to grow the business.
- Repayment of debt. Repaying debt may not be the best way to use surplus cash. Depending on borrowing levels, leverage, business performance and prevailing interest rates, it may be better to retain debt and use the cash to reward equity investors.
- Repayment of equity. This can be in the form of a dividend or a buy-back of shares that makes the remaining shares increase in value.

These options are explained in more detail in Chapters 5 and 6.

Financing strategy

The most common factor determining the size of a business is its financial capacity: the amount of finance it is able to raise. In assessing financial capacity, the most significant attribute used by investors is the forecast of expected cash flows from which an investment can be both serviced and repaid. What investors want to know, therefore, is how much funding the cash flow can comfortably support.

The structure and processes for producing a detailed cash flow forecast were explained in Chapter 2. The resulting profile of cash flow surpluses and deficits for a three-year period enables funding strips to be identified that cover any deficits. It is these funding strips that require financing.

To convince investors that there is adequate cash flow to support the additional finance, the cash flow forecast may need to be extended beyond the three years to cover the duration of the investment.

Borrowing: a return to basic principles

Before the summer of 2008 the world had experienced a decade or more of economic growth fuelled by low interest rates and easy credit. Suddenly the world of banking changed as the foolishness of easy credit became the reality of large-scale default.

From the early days of banking, credit was advanced based on a borrower's ability to service and repay. For secondary protection it was secured by a charge over an asset, typically the asset that was being financed. From the mid-1990s, property prices rose and thus the importance of validating a borrower's ability to pay became secondary to making sure that there was a property asset somewhere in the transaction that would provide the security. All went well for many years: parcels of asset-backed debt were bought and sold in the market, and credit default swaps were taken to cover the unlikely risk that repayment would not materialise. When subprime mortgages (debt to people with poor credit standing and insecure employment) started to default, the banks simply thought that selling the property would clear the debt. But without buyers in the market there was no sale and without a sale there was no ability to repay. It became all too clear that debt secured on overinflated asset values provides no security at all.

As governments stepped in to support and recapitalise the banks, the credit criteria changed. Governments wanted to encourage lending to keep their economies from deep recession and even depression, yet they wanted their banks to focus on low risk. The two requirements are incompatible. Businesses with excellent credit ratings usually have low debt and little need for more; those with poor credit ratings and high debt need refinancing and access to borrowing. This mismatch in what was needed by businesses and what was available from banks led to a Darwinian survival of the fittest and bankruptcy for the rest.

The result of the crisis has been a return to stricter lending criteria with debt granted on the original banking principles: that the amount available is based on the borrower's ability to service and repay, with security taken on conservatively valued assets as a second line of defence in the event that the borrower is unable to pay.

Choosing between debt and equity

Although there is normally clear demarcation between debt capital and equity capital in reality they are quite similar. Relations with both investors and debt providers (like banks) need managing and both require a return and their capital protecting. The difference between the two is in the way this is done and what happens in the event of business failure.

Debt providers typically have a predetermined rate of interest, a defined repayment date and a priority payment position should the business fail.

FIG 3.2 **Relationship between ROI and WACC**

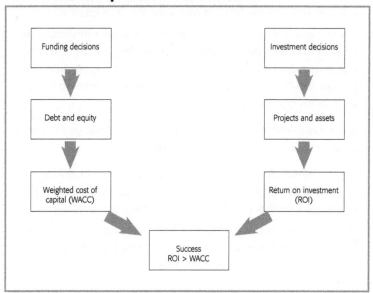

Equity is the money put in by the owners of the business; they are entitled to the profits of the business and therefore a potentially limitless return. The investment is not normally repaid and it is the last to be paid out if the business fails. Equity investors have a much higher risk and potential for reward than debt providers.

In raising funds for a business there needs to be an appropriate balance of debt and equity. The relationship between total debt and total equity is referred to as leverage or gearing. The overall cost of funds, calculated by averaging all the various sources, is known as the weighted average cost of capital (WACC). For a business to be successful, it must generate a return on investment (ROI) that is at least as high as its WACC (see Figure 3.2).

If there is too much debt, a business becomes highly leveraged, with the following implications:

- Repayment risk. The risk to debt providers increases as there is less of an equity buffer to absorb any losses that a business may make.

- Cost. With enhanced risk to debt providers the cost of the loans is likely to rise in the form of increased fees and interest rates.
- Interest risk. The interest cost must be met before dividends can be paid to shareholders. If interest cannot be paid and there is a serious risk of a business not being able to repay its debt, the providers will exercise rights in their loan agreements to force repayment from asset sales.

If there is too little debt, shareholders lose out through dilution of earnings, which limits their return through:

- Greater WACC. As equity is more expensive than debt, the business can lower its WACC by replacing equity with cheaper debt; the enhanced earnings can then be passed back to shareholders.
- Restrained growth. With too little borrowing the business may be operating suboptimally as it has the capacity to borrow more to fund expansion and achieve greater growth.

To prevent businesses from borrowing too much there are covenants in loan agreements that require a business to stay within a range of ratio parameters. Penalties in the form of higher fees, interest rates and even repayment on demand can be required for breaches. Management therefore has to find a way of operating within covenants without damaging the potential of the business. The covenants are in place primarily to protect the banks' investment.

The optimum leverage for a business is seen to be around 50% of total funds. At this level the interest rate on debt is usually unratcheted and the return on equity can be maximised. Figure 3.3 indicates that at high levels of leverage the punitive interest rate charged on the debt significantly reduces the earnings potential for equity investors. As the leverage level drops, the risk to debt providers falls and consequently the interest rate charged falls. With less of the profit being allocated to debt providers, the return to equity investors rises. At low levels of leverage the return on equity falls as the advantage of melding low-rate debt diminishes. The optimum leverage can be seen to be around 50% of total funds.

There are scenarios where a higher level of leverage can be tolerated without the interest rate rising. This might be where a

FIG 3.3 **Return on equity and gearing**

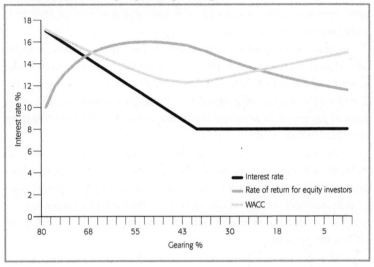

business has a substantial proportion of its assets in an easily tradable form such as property, where the quality of the portfolio enables it to take on greater debt. Assets in the form of specialist machinery are less tradable and therefore provide lower-quality security.

There are many ways of calculating leverage and debt to equity ratios. Options are whether to include or exclude items such as payables, pension deficits and other liabilities. One of the simplest methods is to compare interest-bearing debt to equity. This focuses on pure funding and excludes the operational aspects of the business such as payables. The calculation is as follows:

Debt:equity

This is more easily expressed as a ratio by taking the interest-bearing debt as a proportion of total funds which is calculated as follows:

$$\frac{\text{Interest-bearing debt}}{\text{Equity + interest-bearing debt}} \ \%$$

Equity = share capital + reserves (retained earnings)

The higher the ratio the more highly leveraged is the business. This attracts closer attention from the lending banks to ensure the business can cover its interest payments and can raise the level of control it exercises over the business.

In calculating leverage it is common for lease obligations to be added to the debt amount. This is because the requirement to make a series of payments into the future is similar to servicing a debt. For example, if a leased asset of $1m involves a business making ten annual payments of $150,000 (including interest at 8%), the obligation is similar to having debt equal to the asset value.

Where a business has a significant amount of cash as well as debt, it is sensible to calculate the leverage ratio using net rather than gross debt. For example, a business may have borrowings and cash in different currencies and decide to keep the cash as a hedge against adverse currency movements rather than appear to operate with poor cash management.

The measure is known as net leverage (or net gearing) and is calculated as follows:

$$\frac{\text{Interest-bearing debt} - \text{cash}}{\text{Equity} + \text{interest-bearing debt} - \text{cash}} \ \%$$

As a business makes profits or losses, the level of equity in the business will rise or fall. It therefore needs to monitor the effect of this on leverage. Profits will reduce leverage and provide the business with capacity to take on further borrowings and vice versa. If a business is making high profits, not growing significantly and using surplus cash to repay debt, its leverage can reduce to a suboptimal level. This was the case for oil companies between 2005 and 2008 when large profits were generated from the hike in global oil prices. To avoid suboptimal gearing, it may be preferable to distribute excess profits and cash through share buy-backs or special dividends, thus returning money to equity investors and maintaining leverage and WACC at a more advantageous level.

Rather than cancelling any shares that are bought back, businesses can hold them as treasury stock (which is shown as a negative value under shareholders' equity). Buying back and reselling shares is an efficient way to control leverage and keep the WACC at the optimum point.

Weighted average cost of capital

The WACC is the average funding rate across all the sources of finance. The weighted part refers to the way it is calculated with reference to the proportion that each source of finance contributes to the total.

The WACC is calculated from the returns required by investors from each source of finance, which is derived from factors such as credit rating, leverage, risk-free rates and the way the company's shares correlate to the market as a whole (these are explained in more detail below).

One other factor that will affect equity investors is tax. Interest costs on debt are chargeable against profits for tax calculation purposes and can therefore be used to reduce the tax a business pays. So although debt may have a stated rate of, say, 8%, the actual cost to the equity holders is 8% $\times$ (1 − the tax rate). If tax is chargeable at 30%, the actual cost of debt is as follows:

$$8\% \times (1 - 30\%) = 5.6\%$$

Multiplying the cost of debt by 1 minus the tax rate gives the tax benefit of debt financing to equity investors. This effect is called the tax shield of debt financing.

All the factors affecting the WACC are summarised in Figure 3.4. The formula to calculate WACC can be summarised as follows:

$$\text{WACC} = \frac{(E \times RE)}{(E + D)} + \frac{(D \times RD \times (1 - TR))}{(E + D)}$$

E = market value of equity
RE = return required for equity
D = market value of debt
RD = return required for debt
TR = tax rate

The above formula is too simple for businesses with several sources of debt including bonds, loans, and so on. To complete the calculation each type of debt would be included separately with its own applicable rate. The weighted part is important to ensure that each element added to the formula is included in proportion to the market value of all sources of finance. A way of representing this might be:

FIG 3.4 **Factors affecting the WACC**

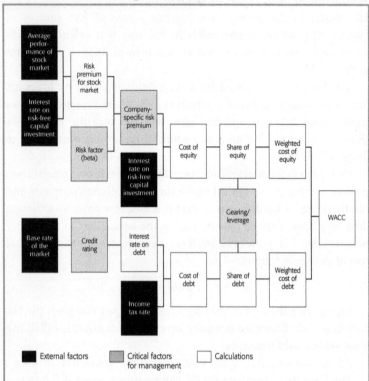

$$WACC = \frac{(E \times RE)}{TF} + \frac{(D_1 \times RD_1 \times (1 - TR))}{TF} + \frac{(D_2 \times RD_2 \times}{TF}$$
$$(1 - TR)) + \frac{(D_3 \times RD_3 \times (1 - TR))}{TF}$$

TF = total market value of all sources of finance
D1 = debt type 1
D2 = debt type 2
D3 = debt type 3

For example, if a company is funded as follows:

Funding source	Amount, $m	Cost of funding, %
Market value of equity	50	12
Market value of bonds	14	9
Market value of an overdraft	1	15
Total	65	

And the tax rate is 30%, the WACC is calculated as:

$$(50/65 \times 12\%) + (14/65 \times (9\% \times 70\%)) + (1/65 \times (15\% \times 70\%)) = 10.75\%$$

A business's WACC is normally kept confidential for commercial reasons. For example, if two companies are seeking to acquire a target business, with all other aspects being equal, the one with the lowest cost of capital will be able to afford to pay the higher price.

Raising debt

When interest rates are low, debt finance can be not only a cost-effective way to finance growth, but also a way to reduce the WACC of the business. With a fixed-rate loan the cost of finance is known and no ownership dilution takes place.

In considering debt finance, be aware of the bank's perspective. The bank's objective in lending is to have a low-risk, profitable transaction. This means it wants customers with a strong cash flow that can service their debt and substantial unencumbered collateral that can cover any default risk (effectively this provides the bank with two means of recovering its loan: trading out and selling out). A bank also wants to charge as high an interest rate as it can justify.

In understanding the bank's objective it becomes clear that there needs to be a negotiation on the detailed terms and conditions of any loan. There is a trade-off between risk and reward. For example, if substantial and broad collateral is available to lower the bank's risk, a lower interest rate can be stipulated. Similarly, a strong cash flow that is evidenced by past performance also lowers the bank's potential risk and can be used to further reduce the interest rate.

In the negotiation a balance has to be struck between driving down the cost of the new debt and leaving capacity for future debt. It can therefore be advantageous to provide as little collateral as possible and, importantly, to make any charge specific to certain assets (such as a property, a piece of equipment, inventory or receivables) rather than general assets. Limiting collateral leaves collateral capacity available for future debt. Debt providers with preferential collateral status are known as senior debt holders and those with little or no collateral are known as junior or subordinate debt holders. As a consequence of the lack of security, junior debt is typically more expensive than senior debt.

Lending requirements

For banks to have the confidence to lend to a business they need a proposal that demonstrates there is low risk of default. They nearly all use a matrix of some form to score the strengths and weaknesses of the proposal. Some of the criteria required are as follows:

- KYC (know your customer). In other words, a bank should understand and assess the business that is taking on the debt and those running it. This is both a validation of their existence and a detailed examination of their experience, track record and even perseverance (evidenced by frequency of employment changes and even divorce). It is the quality of the people that is the most important element; after all, it is the people who will make a success or failure of the venture, not the assets that are purchased with the money provided. Although qualifications and impressive CVs can be included here, the performance of the people in meetings and presentations to the lender will be far more important in conveying confidence. They need to demonstrate passion for the venture, an understanding of the market and a clear strategic vision, and also provide an agile explanation of the financials.
- A proven business with a strong track record. Ideally, the business has taken a loan in the past and can show it paid back interest and capital on due dates. In the absence of this evidence the other criteria will receive greater scrutiny. In a cautious climate new businesses and first-time borrowers may have difficulty in launching their venture. Particular attention will be

paid to the past experience of the directors, and the bank may require equity pledges from the founders to demonstrate their wholehearted commitment as well as to act as buffer for the debt (essentially reducing the leverage).

■ A well-evaluated and robust business plan comprising at least a three-year cash flow forecast, realistic expected financial results and strong evidence for the assumptions that have been used. Forecasts on their own are insufficient; the more important aspect is their sensitivity to a range of scenarios showing they have been thoroughly explored, with "what if" being applied to a wide range of downside attributes such as lower sales revenue, cost increases, delays in getting to market, competitor actions, and so on. For the issues identified there need to be strategies for mitigation.

Loan covenants and monitoring measures

When a bank makes a loan offer there will be conditions attached which are known as loan covenants (contractual restrictions placed upon the borrower). They include a set of monitoring measures used to provide the bank with early warnings of problems. The breaching (or tripping) of a covenant can have significant consequences, including the calling in of the loan itself. Therefore careful monitoring to stay within the criteria is an important part of cash management.

Negotiating more favourable covenants before drawing down the loan is far more effective than trying to change them once a breach has occurred. It should be borne in mind that the bank wants the business to succeed, as this will enable the service and repayment of debt. Therefore any covenant that might restrict the business's success will be in neither party's interest.

Some typical covenants are as follows:

■ Provide regular financial information. This enables the bank to monitor performance and risk.

■ Adhere to certain financial ratios. This covers liquidity (EBITDA and free cash flow multiples), profitability (return on investment and interest cover ratios) and leverage (debt to equity ratios).

- Insurance on both assets and key staff. The loss of these could jeopardise the business and any collateral.
- Pay taxes. To keep the business operating legally.
- Operating restrictions. Permission required for any significant asset purchases or disposals, raising more debt, paying dividends and changing management.

Should a covenant be or be about to be breached it is preferable for the business to advise the bank and discuss options to regularise the situation rather than wait for the bank to identify the breach and intervene more formally. Maintaining a good working relationship with the bank will help find a solution that continues the business rather than jeopardises it. However, frequent or prolonged breaches are likely to result in tighter covenants and penalties in the form of higher interest rates or fees.

Maturity ladders

As a business grows it is likely to use a variety of debt instruments and start to create cash flows that have a predictable element (sales revenue) and an unpredictable element (capital purchases and disposals). It would be unwise for a business to lock itself into long-term debt and then find that it had started generating a substantial cash surplus. Thus a portfolio of debt should be structured with a series of loans that mature over a range of dates. This should also include a small amount of short-term debt (or overdraft) to balance out day-to-day cash receipts and payments. As each part of the debt portfolio matures, any cash that has accumulated can be used to offset the debt, with the net funding requirement carried into a new debt instrument.

Cost of debt funding

In the explanations above some notional figures have been used to illustrate the cost of each funding source and show how these combine to calculate the WACC. It is possible to determine these more scientifically.

International credit agencies such as Moody's and Standard &

FIG 3.5 **Profile of credit increments**

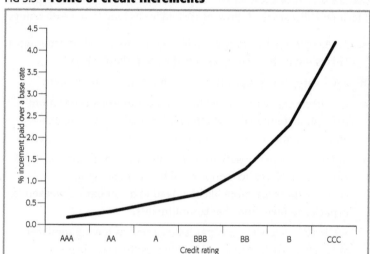

Poor's assess the risk of companies and allocate them a credit rating. A rating of AAA is very low risk and companies in this category pay low rates for their funding. However, a speculative mining company in a politically unstable country is a much greater risk and will expect to pay a much higher cost for its funding. The credit rating typically has an exponential correlation to a premium over a central bank or prime rate of interest. For example, AAA might correlate to 0.25% over the central bank rate, so if the central bank rate is 5%, the debt cost would be 5.25%. However, a rating of BB might be 1.5% over the central bank rate with a debt cost of 6.5%; and a rating of CCC might be 4.5% over the central bank rate with a debt cost of 9.5%. The increments, while remaining exponential, can widen and contract depending on the availability of debt. An illustrative profile of the credit increments is shown in Figure 3.5.

Credit-rating agencies use a range of measures and attributes to calculate their ratings. Ironically, the lower the leverage, the higher is the likely credit rating and the lower the interest rate charged on debt. Using this credit rating advantage to borrow more funds will push up the leverage, reduce the credit rating and increase the interest rate.

Standard & Poor's, an American credit-rating agency that is part of McGraw-Hill, uses the following system for its long-term credit ratings:

- AAA – extremely strong capacity to meet financial commitments. This is the highest rating assigned by Standard & Poor's.
- AA – very strong capacity to meet financial commitments.
- A – strong capacity to meet financial commitments but more susceptible to the adverse effects of changes in circumstances and economic conditions than those in higher-rated categories.
- BBB – adequate capacity to meet financial commitments. However, adverse economic conditions or changing circumstances are more likely to lead to a company's weakened capacity to meet financial commitments.
- BB, B, CCC and CC – companies regarded as having significant speculative characteristics. BB indicates the least degree of speculation and CC the highest. Although such companies are likely to have some quality and protective characteristics, these may be outweighed by large uncertainties or major exposures to adverse conditions.
- D – in default and unable to pay all or substantially all obligations as they come due.
- R – under regulatory supervision owing to financial condition.

A deterioration of one level on this scale increases the interest rate payable and vice versa. Therefore protecting and even improving a credit rating is a critical part of cash management.

Raising equity

The nature of equity capital is that for investors it is riskier than lending money, but it offers a potentially higher return. Thus it can be difficult for a business to get debt finance without there being a sufficient buffer provided by equity investors. This buffer means that if losses arise in the business they will be absorbed initially by the equity investors, giving the debt investors a better chance of getting their capital back.

Consequently, the first stage of raising capital in almost any business will be raising equity. This can come from private investors, such as friends, family or the management of the new business. It will typically be passive investment that gives the management time to build the business. Alternatively, equity can be raised from professional investors such as venture capitalists, which are far from passive in their strategy. They have growth, profit and cash generation targets as well as exit objectives that may have a medium-term horizon such as five years. These ambitions mean that professional investors invest only in businesses that can demonstrate the potential for rapid growth.

The advantages and disadvantages of these two types of initial equity are listed in Table 3.8.

TABLE 3.8 **Private investors versus venture capitalists**

	Private investors	Venture capitalists
Advantages	■ Retain full control ■ No pressure to deliver within a time frame	■ A larger amount of equity available ■ Easier to take on borrowing as banks will respect the rigour of the venture-capital company's analysis and insight ■ Potential for faster growth by having access to larger amounts of cash ■ A clear path to an IPO (see later in this chapter) ■ More clinical decision making
Disadvantages	■ Limited amount of cash available ■ Lack of focus and external guidance at times of need ■ Sentimentality contaminating decisions ■ Difficult for investors to withdraw their investment	■ Dilution of control and a splitting of the ultimate realisation value ■ Lack of patience when progress falls behind schedule

After the initial equity capital has been put in, the next step in funding a business is typically a tranche of debt. The low cost and lack of dilution in control can make this attractive. However, it is wise to delay moving to the first debt stage until the business has started to generate sufficient operating income and cash flow to service the interest payments. An infant business that is highly leveraged when interest rates are rising may find that it quickly breaches covenants and that the interest burden may trigger its premature end.

Once the amount of debt has pushed the leverage to a comfortable limit, the next stage in funding is to seek further equity, which in turn can be used as the basis for further debt. This process then continues as the basis of the funding strategy for long-term growth in the business.

The easiest way to create additional equity is to earn it by being profitable. Retaining the profit in the business, rather than paying it out as dividends, will increase the amount of equity capital in the business. For example, Microsoft, which was started in 1975, reinvested all its profits up until 2003 when its first dividend was declared. This strategy reduced the need for taking on extra borrowing and additional equity capital. The strategy also avoided the dilution of control and thus helped make the founder one of the richest men in the world.

If a business is not generating much in the way of profits, perhaps because of product development, increasing the amount of equity capital requires a call on the existing equity investors; this is known as a rights issue (see below). If the existing equity investors cannot afford to put in additional capital, a wider pool of investors will be needed which may also include venture-capital investors. However, in the absence of a profitable track record it may be difficult to convince this wider pool of investors of the potential within the business.

Once a business has reached a stage where profits and cash flows are growing sustainably, it may be time to take it to market in the form of an initial public offering (IPO). This allows existing shareholders to sell some of their stake in the business and the shares to be traded on an exchange. The expectation at the outset of an IPO is that it will make the founding shareholders wealthy (on paper at least).

It is the prospect of wealth from an IPO that can cause a conflict between the founders and any venture-capital investors. The founders may not like to dilute their control and give up a share of the potential gains, and venture-capital investors typically argue that their involvement will enable the business to grow faster, be more successful and thus worth more, making the founders ultimately better off.

An IPO for a small business may bring its shares onto a junior exchange. As the business grows, it will need to broaden the pool of investors, in particular to attract those that like to see shares more actively traded enabling faster dealing and narrower spreads. This is achieved by moving up to the main market. However, to do this a business will need to be of a certain size as measured by market capitalisation; and, depending upon which exchange the company will be floated, it will need to have been trading for a set number of years, meet working capital requirements and have accumulated a prescribed amount of earnings.

Rights issue

A rights issue is used by a business to sell additional shares to raise further capital. Shares are offered to existing shareholders in proportion to their current shareholding. This pre-emption "right" means that investors can retain their ownership proportion of a business should they choose to. Alternatively, they can sell their right as a tradable security if they do not want to subscribe to the additional shares. If rights are not taken up, the company may (and in practice does) sell them on behalf of the rights holder.

The price at which the new shares are offered is usually at a discount to the current share price, giving investors an incentive to buy the new shares. However, the market price of the company's shares after the new ones have been issued will fall to a weighted average of the original and new shares as follows:

$$\frac{(CP \times ES) + (NP \times NS)}{ES + NS} = \text{Average price of all shares after the rights issue}$$

The attributes are as follows:

- NS is the number of new shares issued for every ES (existing share). For example, if 2 new shares were offered for every 7 existing shares, NS would be 2 and ES would be 7

- CP is the closing price on the last day the original shares were traded with entitlement to the rights issue (known as the cum-rights price)
- NP is the price of each new share

For example, if a share was trading at $2 and a rights issue offered one new share for every two shares held at a price of $1.55, the share price after the offer would become:

$$\frac{(2.00 \times 2) + (1.55 \times 1)}{2 + 1} = 1.85$$

Initial public offering

Taking a business into public ownership is perhaps the most significant decision that founding shareholders will ever make for their company. It therefore requires advice from many sources including accountants, lawyers and investment bankers. While the wealth prospects for the founding shareholders are tempting, there can be substantial drawbacks in floating a business. The management will face far greater scrutiny and relentless demands to provide forecasts, progress reports and explanations for deviations. There are substantial sets of rules to be complied with depending on the country in which and the exchange on which the company's shares will trade. There are also strict codes for corporate governance and compliance with rules such as Sarbanes Oxley in the US. The aim of this section is not to cover all this in detail but to explain the context and process of using an IPO to raise cash.

Once the decision to go for an IPO has been made, the four main aims are to:

- maximise the success of the flotation by securing a quality shareholder base with a full take-up of all the shares offered;
- optimise the price at which the new shares are sold;
- create a stable and rising aftermarket;
- provide trading liquidity and quality research coverage.

The first two are intrinsically related: if the share price is set too low, the share offer may well be oversubscribed; and if it is set too high, it may attract insufficient interest. It is therefore essential to prepare the business for the IPO so that it can present its past achievements and future potential in a way that will attract interest and investment. This can take at least six months, so it is not a quick method of raising cash. Typical requirements are as follows:

- Construct the board (executive and non-executive directors) with appropriate depth and breadth to provide confidence in the potential of the business.
- Prepare a prospectus that will include:
    - summary of the IPO
    - risk factors
    - description of the business (what it does)
    - operating and financial review (how the business operates and its strategy for income and capital growth)
    - audited accounts for the past three years
    - working capital statement to demonstrate the business has sufficient cash to last at least 12 months
    - other information such as the details of the board, dividend policy and terms of the share issue.
- Complete due diligence to ensure the accuracy and completeness of the prospectus.
- Complete a valuation of the business to identify the target price at which the business will be floated.
- Brief analysts so that they understand the IPO and can inform the investor community of its arrival.
- Target key investors.

To ensure the success of an IPO it is normal to have the whole issue underwritten, which means that institutions will guarantee to take up any unsold stock. The benefit of underwriting is that the full amount of capital sought is raised, but at a price. An IPO is an expensive way to raise cash as a business must not only pay for the contributions of a large group of advisers, but also commit senior management time and resources.

There are also fees to be paid once the company has floated. Underwriting, professional advice and listing fees would be around 10% of the capital raised for an IPO of $50m: that is, 3% for underwriting (typically up to 6% in the United States), 3–6% for advisers and 1% for listing. The underwriting fee is usually a percentage of the amount of capital sought. However, with advisers' fees the more capital raised the lower is the percentage; there is an economy of scale effect for the production of a prospectus.

As well as the direct cost there is the indirect cost of lost capital by underpricing on the day of sale. This share price discount is calculated on the first day of trading. If the shares rise 10% on day one, then although shareholders will be delighted with their new investment, it is 10% more capital that the business could have raised if the strike price had been set at a higher level.

Once the IPO is complete there are further costs, including maintaining the register of shareholders as trades are completed, paying dividends, publishing reports and accounts at least annually (or quarterly for a main listing). Although many companies put most of their shareholder communications online to reduce the costs of printing and postage, it can still cost up to 3% of the funds to manage the group of investors (depending on the amount of funds and the fragmentation of the shareholder base).

Investor relations

The purpose of investor relations is to attract and retain investment funds and thus ensure the share price remains a fair reflection of the company's worth. An undervalued company soon becomes the target of a takeover.

Investor relations involves dialogue with the investment community, listening to feedback and presenting plans for capital growth and returns. The communication is both regulatory and voluntary and normally serves four groups:

- Institutional investors. Institutions such as pension funds, insurance companies and unit trusts are likely to take up the majority of shares in a listed company. Their investment intentions are long term so the retention of their funds is paramount in building a stable shareholder base. Their objective is to achieve best value for their investors so they need to be convinced of the long-term value-creation prospects of the business.

■ Private investors. Although these can be numerous, the combined value of their individual holdings is often insignificant. Employees and some private investors can be a loyal group of investors but expensive to manage and communicate with.

■ Analysts. A group of individuals that complete financial analysis on a company's performance and expresses options on its potential. A buy or sell recommendation from a leading investment bank can prompt large movements in shares and thus affect the share price. There are two types of analyst: those working on the sell side for an investment bank (who publish research to help influence investors); and those working on the buy side for a fund manager (who originate private research to support internal stock selection).

■ Media. It is as important to promote the corporate brand as it is to publicise financial performance. Media coverage attracts interest in a company and affects both investment and sales.

It should be remembered that the equity investors own the business and that the board of directors is accountable to them. The owners want to know how their investment has performed and what the board thinks are the business's prospects for the future. If the owners are unhappy with the way directors keep them informed, they have the power to fire them.

Cost of equity

To calculate the return required by investors the capital asset pricing model (CAPM) is used. This compares the return made on a risk-free investment with two factors: the overall return that is expected from the market and how well the business will be able to match the market.

Required return = risk-free return + beta (expected market return − risk-free return)

- A risk-free return is usually deemed to be a government bond where the investor is confident of both the interest and capital repayment.
- The market return is calculated by reference to one of the composite stockmarket indexes, which provides the average return from investing in, say, the top 100 companies.
- Beta is a coefficient that is used to quantify the risk of this investment compared with the risk-free return and the average market return. If the risk is greater than the average market risk, a higher than average market return will be demanded and vice versa.

A beta is calculated using regression analysis to measure how well aligned the company's share performance will be to movement in the market as a whole:

- A beta of 1 indicates that a business's performance will be synchronised with the market.
- A beta of less than 1 indicates that a business's performance will be less volatile than the market.
- A beta greater than 1 indicates that a business's performance will be more volatile than the market.

For example, if a company has a beta of 1.1, it is theoretically 10% more volatile than the market.

Defensive companies, such as utility companies and some food manufacturers, typically have a beta of less than 1. High-tech companies typically have a more volatile return, more risk and a beta greater than 1.

Using the CAPM model and some assumptions the required return can be calculated:

Risk-free rate	5%
Expected market return	9%
Beta for the investment	1.2

Therefore the required return to the equity holders is:

5% + 1.2 (9% − 5%) which equates to 9.8%

The implication of the theory is that the more a business performs like the market the lower is the required return. Consequently, the more unique and radical a business becomes the higher is the return that investors will require. This may discourage entrepreneurship in favour of the tried and tested.

Hedging interest-rate and foreign-exchange rate risks

Hedging is a way of managing financial risk. The risk is that interest rates and/or exchange rates move adversely resulting in reduced profits. These risks can be minimised or fixed, but there is a cost and the potential to lose out on the benefit of any favourable movements in rates.

Hedging interest rate risk

As explained above, debt capital can often fund around 50% of a business and thus a rise in interest rates, even if only 1%, can have a significant impact on overall profitability. Therefore limiting the impact of potential interest-rate rises can be as important to a business's bottom line as pay settlements and price rises.

In its simplest form hedging can be done by taking out a loan or issuing a bond with a fixed rather than a floating rate of interest. This fixed rate provides certainty of the interest cost for the life of the debt. However, the interest rate applied to the debt will be related to the prevailing bank rate at the time the cash is raised, which is unlikely to coincide with the bottom of the cycle of rises and falls in interest rates. If, for example, the debt is for ten years, having a fixed rate may avoid higher rates for several of those years, but the business may fail to benefit from lower rates for other years. Thus more sophisticated instruments are needed to protect the downside of interest rate rises and yet allow the upside of interest-rate falls. These are called derivatives – products where the value and characteristics are derived from another product. They include caps, collars and swaps.

Base-rate cap

A base-rate cap is designed to restrict the cost of interest-rate rises but retain the benefit of interest-rate falls. It is a separate product from a

FIG 3.6 **A base-rate cap**

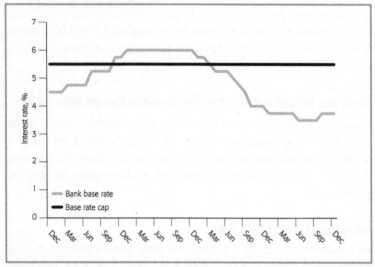

loan, though it is normally taken out in conjunction with a floating-rate bank loan. The base-rate cap takes the form of a legal agreement for a notional amount of capital at a fixed-cap rate of interest for a set period of time – for example, $5m at a capped rate of 5.5% for five years. There is an upfront fee for setting up the agreement.

During the five-year period the business will be susceptible to changes in interest rates on its floating-rate loan and the full interest will have to be paid. The separate base-rate cap means that the counterparty (usually a bank) will pay the business any excess over the average base rate that is above the agreed cap rate. In the example, whenever the base rate exceeds 5.5% the difference between the average base rate and 5.5% will be paid quarterly to the business. The net effect is that the business is protected from higher interest rates. Because a base-rate cap is a separate financial product from a loan, if there is surplus cash in the business the loan can be repaid (avoiding interest altogether) and the base-rate cap will endure for its contractual term. In Figure 3.6, the cap would come into effect for the period where the base rate exceeds 5.5%.

FIG 3.7 **A base-rate collar**

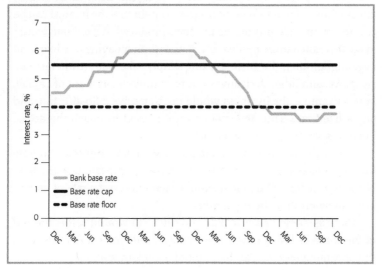

Base-rate collar

This is a similar product to a base-rate cap in that it defines the maximum (cap) interest rate to be paid, but it also adds a base-rate floor that defines the lowest (floor) interest rate that the business may benefit from. If interest rates fall below the floor, the business pays the bank the difference between the average base rate and the agreed floor rate. The benefit of this product is that the upfront premium is much less than for a base-rate cap. In Figure 3.7, the cap would come into effect for the period where base rate exceeds 5.5% and the business would receive interest. The floor would come into effect below 4% and the business would have to pay interest.

Base-rate swap

A base-rate swap is used to convert a floating-rate debt into a fixed-rate debt and vice versa. As with the base-rate cap and collar, this is a separate transaction from the debt itself. The two parties (usually a business and a bank) agree to swap the interest payments and the cash flows are normally settled as a net transaction of the difference between the two rates.

For example, a business may have floating-rate borrowings and on the purchase of equipment wants to be certain that the interest can be covered by the margins on the products produced. A fixed rate would make this much more predictable. Rather than repaying one loan and negating another, the business can simply take out an interest-rate swap. As with other derivatives it is for a notional amount of capital. In this example, the business would opt to receive a floating rate and pay a fixed rate. Thus the swap receipt is used to match the actual interest payment on the actual debt.

Although this may sound straightforward, it is important to note that swap rates are priced relative to a base rate prevailing at the time of the transaction. Thus the fixed-rate element is not a rate of choice, but one determined by the market.

These agreements are flexible and can be unwound before the end of the contract, though there is normally a settlement value based on the prevailing base rate at the point of early termination.

Forward rate agreement

A forward rate agreement (FRA) is a way of setting up the interest rate to be paid on a short-term notional loan that will be drawn at a future date. As with the previous derivatives, the FRA is used to set interest-rate parameters and the loan itself is a separate transaction.

For example, a construction business may need to take out a loan in three months' time to purchase a large amount of inventory that it will have to carry for six months before it receives payment from its customer. It may also need to fix the selling price of the transaction in advance, so the margins on the contract will be susceptible to changes in the interest cost of the loan. An FRA can be used to fix the rate today for the future loan and therefore secure the contract's profitability.

In this example a 3×9 FRA might be used. This means the interest is fixed today (the trade date) on a notional loan starting in three months' time (the settlement date) and ending in nine months' time. The FRA is set with a rate at the time of the trade. Cash settlement takes place at end of the forward part (the three months) and will be for the notional amount multiplied by the change in rates from the trade date to the fixing date (normally two days before the settlement date) for the six months of the loan.

Other derivatives

Many more derivative instruments can be used such as futures, options and swap options, known as swaptions. These provide the borrower with various ways to hedge interest-rate risk for a period of time that starts either at the point of the transaction or at a future date.

While the concept and benefit of these derivatives may be clear, many of the finer details of these transactions are complicated to understand and difficult to account for. It is easy to make errors in implementation; for example, if the dates for the derivates do not align with the underlying debt, there can be interest-rate exposure for the period of mismatch, even if it is only one day.

Hedging foreign-exchange-rate risk

The effects of exchange rates on transactions in foreign currencies can be favourable or unfavourable. They arise in two ways:

■ At a transactional level where a business buys and sells products or services in one currency but operates in another; for example, a retailer who imports products from another country.

■ At an investment level where a business has assets or liabilities based abroad and denominated in a different currency from the one in which it accounts for its business; for example, a branch of a business that is based abroad or a multinational where an organisation has operations and businesses around the world.

There are a number of hedging techniques that can be used to protect a business from losses caused by adverse currency movements.

Transactions

When transacting with a business in another country, the potential for foreign-exchange gains and losses arises as a result of differences between the exchange rate on the date the transaction was recorded and the exchange rate on the date the cash is received or paid. For example:

- A UK business sells $1,500 of goods to a US customer when the exchange rate is $1.5:£1.
- The sale is recorded as $1,500/1.5 = £1,000 in the UK company's income statement.
- There is a period of 30 days before the customer has to settle the account during which time the dollar weakens to $1.6:£1.
- The amount received is therefore $1,500/1.6 = £937.50.
- The difference between the £1,000 originally recorded and the £937.50 received represents a foreign-exchange loss and is taken to the income statement as part of the operating income for the year.

This type of foreign-exchange gain or loss can arise on a number of transactions, such as importing raw materials, buying services and exporting goods.

The simplest way to eliminate such exchange-rate movements is to trade with businesses in other countries in your business's base currency. In the example above this would be achieved by raising an invoice in sterling for £1,000. The exchange-rate risk is therefore taken by the buyer. While this may seem simple, it is easier to apply when you are the buyer rather than the seller. Exchange-rate risk is more common on the sales side of a business as the transaction is often set up to meet customer demands.

Forward contract

A forward contract is a contractual agreement that fixes the exchange rate on a sum of money at a future date. There is a fee for this service and loss of any potential foreign-exchange gain, but there is no downside loss. The forward contract would be purchased at the point of sale to fix the rate at which the proceeds will be converted back to the base currency.

Currency future

A currency future is an agreement between two parties – a buyer and a seller – to buy or sell a particular currency at a future date at a particular exchange rate that is fixed. Although this is the same as a forward contract, it is structured as a tradable contract that can be bought or sold on a futures exchange. Therefore if the exchange rates are moving advantageously the currency future can be sold, leaving the business unhedged but able to take advantage of any further favourable movements.

One problem with forward contracts and currency futures is that there is no potential for taking the gain in favourable exchange-rate movements. This is the benefit of options.

Currency option

A currency option is where the purchaser of the option has the right, but not the obligation, to buy or sell a currency at a specific exchange rate at or before a specific date. A call option gives the buyer the right to buy a specified currency at a specified exchange rate. A put option gives the buyer the right to sell a specified currency at a specified exchange rate.

As with other derivative exchange-rate products, there is a fee (or premium) for this contract. If exchange rates move unfavourably, the option can be exercised to cover the losses. However, if exchange rates move favourably, the option can be left to lapse and no settlement takes place.

Assets and liabilities

For overseas investments, hedging techniques can be used to mitigate some of the foreign-exchange risk. A common technique is to borrow money in the same currency as the investment and try to match the amount of borrowing to the value of the net investment. Thus as exchange rates move the exchange gains made on the net investment are matched by an equal exchange loss on the borrowing, and vice versa.

For example, a UK company makes an investment of £500,000 in the US, borrowing in dollars when the rate was $2:£1. This gives an initial investment and borrowing of $1m.

	£	Exchange rate	$
Net investment	500,000	2:1	1,000,000
Borrowing	500,000	2:1	1,000,000

One year later the exchange rate has moved to $1.8:£1. The UK value of the US investment has changed from £500,000 to £555,556. There are no foreign-exchange gains or losses as the gain on the investment is exactly matched by the loss on the borrowing.

	$	Exchange rate	£
Net investment	1,000,000	1.8:1	555,556
Borrowing	1,000,000	1.8:1	555,556

Some governments impose tight operating constraints on overseas investment by, for example:

■ not allowing profits to be remitted out of the country so any surpluses have to be reinvested back in the business;
■ encouraging further inward investment of the profits by levying withholding tax, typically between 10% and 15%, on any remittance out of the country.

Businesses should explore the funding environment thoroughly before identifying the funding source. Even with careful planning, it is impossible to predict the actions of future governments on investment in their country.

4 Working capital efficiency

IN MOST BUSINESSES the staff focus on managing the operations and trying to provide good customer service rather than on the cash flow position. Thus they may:

- buy inventory ahead of time to avoid it running out;
- keep plenty of inventory on the shelves just in case customers should want it;
- let customers have extended credit to help retain their loyalty;
- pay suppliers promptly to encourage them to provide a good service in return.

None of these actions will help cash flow, in fact quite the opposite. Therefore operational effectiveness involves increasing the quality of customer service while minimising the amount of cash that has to be invested in the working capital to serve them.

Working capital consists of three areas that require careful management:

- Payables. The money due to suppliers for goods and services received. The speed of payment determines the rate at which cash leaves the business.
- Inventory. The holding of goods whether raw materials, work in progress (WIP) or finished goods. The amount of inventory determines the amount of cash tied up.
- Receivables. The money due from customers once products and services have been delivered. The speed of receipt determines the rate at which cash arrives into the business.

FIG 4.1 **The working capital cycle**

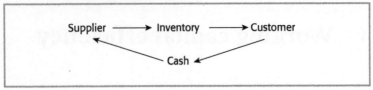

There is often debate about whether cash should be included or excluded as part of working capital. As cash is not "working" in the business, it is normally excluded from working capital thus limiting the definition to just the three trading items.

The working capital cycle in Figure 4.1 shows that cash enters the cycle when a supplier is paid and is released when a customer pays. The aim is therefore to minimise the period of time that cash is tied up in the cycle. The longer the period of time, the greater is the amount of cash required from investors.

In managing the working capital cycle an ideal scenario is to have what is known as negative working capital. This is where cash is received from customers in advance of cash being paid to suppliers and thus working capital becomes a source of rather than an investment of cash. Food retailers typically manage to achieve this because their customers pay cash (or cash equivalents), which eliminates receivables, their inventory is low since much of it is perishable, and they pay suppliers at least a month after receiving cash from their customers.

Although working capital is minimised by keeping inventory low, collecting cash from customers promptly and deferring payments to suppliers, these all hinge on other activities such as setting customer credit limits, establishing contract terms, knowing the customer purchasing procedure, prompt invoicing, and so on. If each element in the chain is improved, the more substantial the cash improvement is likely to be. This chapter explores a wide range of steps that help minimise working capital and which can also enhance customer service. Three stages are involved:

- Purchase to payment – the steps from placing an order with a supplier through to the receipt of goods or services and payment of the supplier's invoice.

- Inventory management – the conversion, storage and movement of goods as they progress from the receipt of raw materials to the delivery of the finished product to the final consumer.

- Order to cash – the steps from receiving a customer order through to the delivery of goods or services and collecting the customer's cash.

Funding working capital

Although cash might take only a few weeks or months to complete the working capital cycle, this does not mean that the overall investment made in working capital is equally short-term. For example, inventory may be constantly moving with items being purchased and sold each day, yet there will be an underlying average level of residual (or safety) inventory being permanently carried. This residual inventory is effectively a constant investment, for which long-term funding could be suitable.

A typical inventory profile is shown in Figure 4.2. Daily sales range from zero to 30 units. Inventory is purchased once a week. The amount acquired not only replaces the inventory sold, but also anticipates the sales likely to be made in the following week. The overall inventory level ranges from a low of 20 units (just before replenishment) to a high of 110 units (just after replenishment), with an average holding of around 70 units. This average level of inventory has to be maintained and funded throughout the year.

Reducing the inventory to run at a lower average level will reduce the cash tied up, but of course risks the business running out of a product and forgoing a sale. However, the saving in inventory funding may be much greater than the lost profit from a few lost sales. There is a balance to be struck between maximising sales and minimising inventory.

The same underlying principles apply to the average level of receivables and payables. While the amounts will change on a daily basis, the net amount of inventory plus receivables less payables is

FIG 4.2 **An inventory profile**

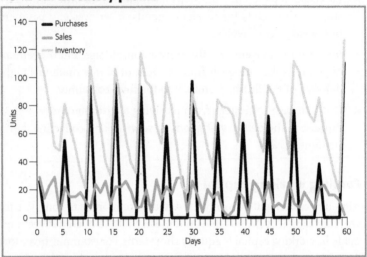

in effect a long-term investment. The average net balance of working capital should therefore be funded with long-term finance that can be raised at a lower interest rate than would be available for short-term funding. However, peaks and troughs will occur – especially in seasonal businesses – for which shorter-term finance can be used to avoid carrying the long-term funding cost when operating at lower levels.

Where funding for a business is proving difficult to raise there are opportunities to reduce working capital by means of vendor-managed inventory (VMI), factoring receivables and other techniques that are explained later in the chapter.

If management want to grow the business (by increasing daily sales), this will inevitably raise the level of working capital in the business. This is because, for example, the level of inventory that is held will be increased to avoid the risk of having stock outs, and the net increase in receivables less payables will have to be funded. Therefore as growth increases the amount of cash tied up in working capital increases, and any restrictions on business funding can become a constraint on growth. The opposite is also true; a contraction in business activity will reduce the level of working capital that needs to be held which releases cash to the rest of the business.

If growth is carefully planned and controlled, the funding of the incremental working capital can be similarly planned. However, when growth occurs unexpectedly, there may be no finance in place to fund additional working capital. In the absence of sufficient cash flow, delays in settling payables become the only way to fund the increase in inventory. At this point the business enters a phase of what is known as overtrading, which has a huge appetite for cash. Investment is required to fund the increase in working capital and to enable supplier terms to be met.

Measuring and monitoring working capital levels

Although the level of working capital can have a huge influence on cash flow, it is rare to find it included as one of the main organisational measures. Sales volume, revenue, return on investment, earnings per share and a range of profit measures are often seen to have far more importance and focus. It is typical to find that only the people in warehouse operations, credit control and accounts payable (who process the transactions) regularly see the working capital balances, yet everyone in the business has an ability to influence the levels. For example, quality control is important in ensuring that there is no excuse for payment delays on the grounds that one item in a batch is substandard. Or, if a sales person hears that a customer is laying off staff, this may mean the company is in trouble and credit control should be encouraged to chase payment of any outstanding invoices.

By involving everyone in the business in the management of working capital it is possible that substantial cash flow advantages can be gained. A clear measurement process is required to monitor levels of each item and corrective actions taken when adverse movements occur.

The common measures used to monitor the level of working capital items are day measures: payables is measured by the number of days a business waits before settling its accounts with suppliers; inventory is measured by the number of days it is held for resale; and receivables is measured by the number of days it takes to collect cash. Payable days is calculated as:

$$\frac{\text{Payables}}{\text{Cost of sales}} \times 365$$

Inventory days is calculated as:

$$\frac{\text{Inventory}}{\text{Cost of sales}} \times 365$$

Receivable days is calculated as:

$$\frac{\text{Receivables}}{\text{Revenue}} \times 365$$

In each of these measures the denominator reflects an annual level of activity in the same terms as the numerator. For example, inventory excludes profit and so cost of sales is the best approximation to annual level of inventory consumption. Also any sales or value-added taxes should be removed from the receivables and payables so that both sides of the equation are exclusive of tax.

Where business volumes are growing or shrinking significantly the calculation based on annual activity can be misleading: it will overstate the average number of days when the business is growing and understate it when it is contracting. In such situations it can be more appropriate to use activity either over the last two months and multiply by 60 or over the last three months and multiply by 90.

Table 4.1 illustrates the day measures that might be experienced in two different industries.

TABLE 4.1 **Day measures in different industries, days**

	Engineering	**Food retail**
Inventory	75	10
Receivables	50	0
Payables	60	45
Working capital cycle	65	−35

Table 4.1 shows the advantage of a cash business, such as food retailing, that eliminates receivables. However, the challenge for a

FIG 4.3 **The net trading cycle**

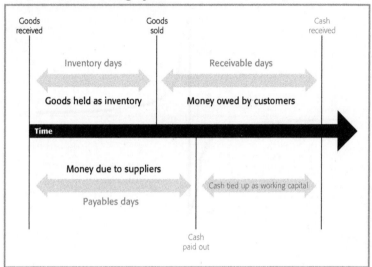

retailer is to turn inventory into cash before suppliers have to be paid and thus sustain negative working capital (see above). Engineering is typical of many manufacturing industries that require substantial working capital (in this example being equivalent to two months' trading) to operate. This net cycle is shown in Figure 4.3.

Another way to measure the cycle is working capital turnover, which is calculated as:

$$\frac{\text{Revenue}}{\text{Inventory} + \text{trade receivables} - \text{trade payables}}$$

The result is a value that is a multiple. As working capital becomes leaner the multiple will increase. However, this will not always be true, as Figure 4.4 shows.

Starting on the right-hand side of the chart, as a business lowers the amount of working capital (on the horizontal axis) the working capital turnover increases, illustrating the efficiency that has been gained. If the business manages to reduce working capital still further until it becomes negative, additional improvements will be achieved through a decrease in the ratio showing that more cash has been released.

FIG 4.4 **Working capital turnover**

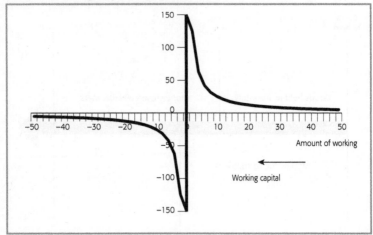

Impact of inflation

Inflation can have a dramatic impact on the diminishing value of cash during the collection of accounts receivable. For example, if products or services are invoiced at $100 and collected from the customer two months later, there would appear to be no loss. If inflation is running at, say, 24%, the purchasing power of the cash will have fallen by at least 4% during the period of credit. If 4% is the net margin on the products or services, effectively there was a zero gain from the transaction. While developed economies have enjoyed a substantial period of low inflation this effect has been almost ignored, but with inflation heading upwards it will again become a factor to consider, as it has been for businesses in a number of developing economies. In times of high inflation cash on delivery should be used instead of providing credit.

The purchase to payment cycle: managing payables

The purchase to pay (sometimes known as P2P) or buying cycle has five distinct stages (see Figure 4.5). It starts with supplier identification and potentially a bidding process to select a preferred supplier. The purchase-order process authorises and requisitions supplies. This is

FIG 4.5 **The purchase to payment cycle**

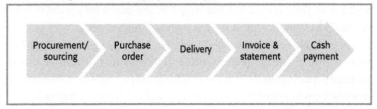

followed by delivery, invoicing and payment. The aim is to seek not necessarily the lowest-price supplier but the supplier that, taking price and service elements into account, provides the best overall value.

Procurement/sourcing

The primary role of those responsible for procurement is to obtain goods and services in response to internal needs. This requires an understanding of the business's requirements and then seeking products and services at the right price, from the right source, in the right quantity and to the right specification.

Their role also encompasses a strategic perspective. They should:

- monitor supply markets and trends (such as material price increases, shortages, changes in suppliers) and interpret the impact of these trends;
- identify the critical materials and services required to support the business;
- develop supply options and contingency plans.

To fulfil this they must identify potential suppliers, complete background reviews including capability and reliability, handle any tendering process, complete negotiations and set up supply agreements.

One essential element of the supply agreement that will affect cash management will be the payment terms. Ideally, the payment period should be as long as possible, but in negotiation there will often be a balance between price and payment terms. Usually the price discussion is the priority for purchasing managers wanting to demonstrate they have derived best value. However, for a business where cash flow is strained, the length of the payment period will be the main benefit, even if it means paying a higher price.

As well as seeking extended payment terms for goods, it helps to delay the purchase of the products until just before the point of use. If the product arrives and sits on a shelf for 30 days, some of the benefit of extended credit is lost. (This is covered under inventory below.)

To manage a supply chain effectively the critical suppliers should be engaged with the shared aim of a long-term, mutually beneficial supply agreement. A business that pushes suppliers as hard as possible by negotiating the most advantageous terms will undoubtedly strain relationships and potentially jeopardise the long-term objective.

In every instance, it should go without saying that contracts should be free of any taint of cronyism or corruption; indeed, legislation in several countries concerning this has been tightened up.

Purchase order
Supplier reliability

The more unreliable a supplier, the greater is the need to order in advance and hold additional safety inventory. To keep safety inventory levels low, it is necessary to look at two supplier factors:

- Response time. The lead time from a supplier receiving an order and fulfilling it. Sourcing supplies from another continent to drive down cost may be advantageous at one level but is likely to extend lead time (for transport) and require higher inventory levels to cover for uncertainty and potential delays.

- Delivery performance. The likelihood of delivery failure as a result of, say:
    - supplier error – failures in fulfilling an order to specification;
    - short or delayed delivery – the inability to supply on time and in full, which is critical in supplier performance;
    - product quality – damaged, not to specification, or not fit for purpose.

Demand forecasting

Over-ordering means cash is unnecessarily tied up in inventory; under-ordering may mean sales are lost. Therefore demand forecasting is essential to provide the basis for supply quantities. A forecast is normally derived from historical data samples and market intelligence. The volatility of demand from an average level will be accommodated by using the safety inventory.

An important additional calculation is forecast bias. This is the cumulative sum of under- or over-forecasting over a period of time. If, for example, a sales force has a habit of being too bullish in its sales forecasts, the result will be overstocking and corrections can be made to future forecasts.

A good process for demand forecasting collects information as far down the supply chain as possible, for example at the order rather than the sale stage. Seasonal patterns must also be taken into account.

There are numerous different forecasting packages available, all of which use combinations of mathematical models to simulate and predict the future demand (see Chapter 2).

Economic order quantity

Small, frequent orders may reduce inventory but increase costs because they do not qualify for volume discounts. To counter this, a call-off contract can be established, whereby an annual purchase volume is agreed with a volume discount and orders are "called off" as required. This type of deal is only appropriate for products or services where an annual level of demand can be predicted with reasonable certainty. The advantage to the supplier of having a confirmed order for a year's supply is that it allows the supplier some flexibility to build inventory at slack times for storage until it is called off.

For less predictable supplies, the following economic order quantity (EOQ) formula can be used to evaluate the appropriate purchase quantity.

$$EOQ = \sqrt{\frac{2RS}{CI}}$$

Where:

R = Annual usage of an item

S = Ordering cost (in total not per unit)

C = Unit cost

I = Holding cost per unit for one year

For example:

Annual demand	3,000 units
Average order cost	$20
Item cost	$12
Average holding cost	25%

Applying this through the formula would suggest the economic order quantity is:

$$\sqrt{\frac{2 \times 3000 \times 20}{12 \times 25\%}} = 200 \text{ units}$$

Figure 4.6 shows the relationship between holding cost and order cost. The lowest point of the total cost line identifies the optimum order quantity, which is 200.

This formula calculates a reorder quantity (ROQ), but some inventory systems also require a reorder level (ROL). This is the amount of remaining stock at which an order will be placed. There is a balance between running the stock too low with the risk of missing a sale and being overcautious and ordering too early. (This is covered in the section below on reducing safety inventory.)

In principle, the typical strategy on EOQ is that:

■ high-value items should be ordered often while maintaining low inventory levels;

■ low-value items should be ordered infrequently while holding higher inventory levels.

FIG 4.6 **Relationship between holding cost and order cost**

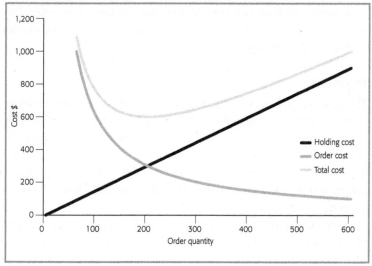

Delivery

The physical arrival of a product is usually accompanied by a delivery note. This is the document that, once signed on receipt of goods, will trigger the supplier to send an invoice and start the countdown to payment. The narrower the gap the purchaser can arrange between accepting delivery and using the product or service the better.

Invoices

Invoices are the inputs into the accounting system that will lead to payments of cash out of the business. Supplier statements provide a summary of the invoices received. It is important to carefully check invoices submitted for payment to ensure that only valid payments are made. Typical errors involve quantities, prices, credit terms, taxation treatment and even the arithmetic. Although the matching of electronic purchase orders to supply agreements can be automated, simple common-sense checks should be used to challenge all large amounts or frequent items (to make sure that multiple invoicing of the same item has not taken place).

Once an invoice is confirmed as valid it should be authorised for payment. The principle of segregation of duties should be used here to separate the buyer or orderer from the payment authoriser. This makes it more difficult for someone to approve a fictitious invoice and defraud the business.

Payment

The physical payment should be made in accordance with the terms set out in the supply agreement. Stretching these terms risks damaging the relationship with the supplier and disrupting future supplies. However, if cash is short it may be advantageous to renegotiate terms, if only on a temporary basis. To pay part of the outstanding balance can help maintain supplies until the full outstanding balance can be cleared.

Obviously, payment should only be made once, but errors happen all too often. Therefore strong automated controls are needed to prevent duplicating payments and to flag potential issues for detailed checking. Such controls include checking whether invoice numbers are repeated, identical amounts are paid to the same supplier, and purchase-order numbers are referenced more than once.

Where the business is large, has a good credit rating and has a lot of smaller suppliers perhaps with weaker credit ratings, it can offer these suppliers an invoice discounting scheme. This will allow the business to avoid accelerating payments out, but will enable suppliers to accelerate their cash in.

The basis of the scheme is that a business advises a bank of the money due to a supplier and the date payment will be made. If the supplier wants the money faster, it can have it less the cost of interest for the period from when the bank pays out to when the bank receives the cash on the due date. The benefit of this scheme is that it enables the supplier to have a cost of interest based on the business's good credit rating rather than its own poorer credit rating.

The inventory cycle

The inventory cycle is the efficient movement of products from suppliers to customers (or in a wider context supply chain management, encompassing costs, manpower, warehousing, inventory and other

FIG 4.7 **The inventory cycle**

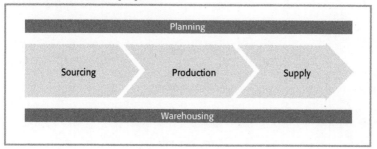

activities). This chapter looks only at the inventory implications as this is where the cash is tied up. For a more detailed understanding of supply chain activities see *The Economist Guide to Supply Chain Management* by David Jacoby.

The inventory cycle connects purchasing and supplying and is dependent on the anticipation and satisfaction of customer demand achieved by timely ordering and supply – minimising the duration of warehousing in this process is one of the main ways of reducing inventory levels.

Inventory is a consequence of trading in products. It can be in the form of raw materials, work in progress (WIP) and finished goods ready for sale. There can also be spare parts operations for businesses such as carmakers. A business holds inventory for the following reasons:

- as a buffer to manage uncertainty in supply such as lead times, quality and order fulfilment;
- to purchase in economic order quantities;
- to ensure continuous production runs with a complete set of components;
- to cope with unpredictable demand and the desire not to pass up a sales opportunity;
- to provide customer choice.

The aim is to reduce inventory because it not only ties up cash in the business but also exposes it to other financial costs that destroy cash, such as:

FIG 4.8 **Profile of inventory**

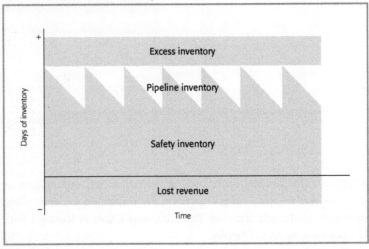

- storage – the cost of warehouse space, warehouse staff and any particular storage conditions (such as chilled storage or secure storage);
- management – the cost of management time in counting, finding, moving and inspecting;
- obsolescence – the risk that inventory will become unsaleable if held for too long or because product enhancements are required;
- damage – the inventory has the potential to become unsaleable;
- theft – the removal of inventory.

Inventory is often held "just in case", usually because replenishment has elements of unreliability or demand is inconsistent. Thus the efficient management of inventory depends on appropriate planning and the skilful management of supplier and customer relationships aimed at increasing certainty in both supply and demand.

The profile of inventory is summarised in Figure 4.8, with time on the horizontal axis and the level of inventory on the vertical axis. The four separate areas are described in Table 4.2.

TABLE 4.2 **The four inventory areas**

	Explanation	**Improvement opportunities**
Pipeline inventory	The peaks represent inventory arriving after which sales cause it to fall. The trough is the point when a reorder brings inventory back to its peak level	More frequent and smaller orders reduce pipeline inventory. This may push up supply costs if the business loses out on volume discounts and incurs higher delivery charges (see economic order quantity to calculate optimum order frequency and order size)
Safety inventory	Buffer inventory allows sales to be made when demand and/or supply is uncertain. The level of uncertainty dictates the amount of safety inventory that needs to be held	A combination of improved demand forecasting and supplier reliability – the latter usually has the greatest impact
Lost revenue	The sales that could have been made if inventory had been available	Investigation of specific unfulfilled orders and lapsed accounts to determine the consequences regarding long-term customer behaviour
Excess inventory	The needless holding of inventory that wastes resources	Improved inventory planning

Managing the portfolio

As a manufacturing business grows it can develop a complex portfolio of products, variants, components, spares and subassemblies. The number of separate product items or stock-keeping units (SKUs) determines the range of inventory held. There are several ways in which to reduce the inventory required to support a portfolio.

Simplification and standardisation

The first stage is to simplify the range of products and components that are held by, for example:

■ having fewer variants in terms of size, colour, flavour, format and so on;

■ standardising components, with different products sharing the same parts – many car manufacturers, for instance, use identical components in different models;

■ single sourcing to reduce safety inventory and make frequent deliveries economical.

Vendor-managed inventory

In this case a supplier retains ownership of inventory and manages its provision within a customer site straight into line side storage areas ready for production. The management of lead times and safety stock remains with the supplier and it is only purchased from the supplier at the point of use. The agreement can allow for penalties should a component not be available when needed.

Sale or return

Where there is uncertainty about the use or sale of a product, the risk can be left with the supplier by a business taking inventory on a sale or return basis. If the product is used it is paid for, and if it is not used it is simply sent back to the supplier. This is an efficient way to trial new product ideas and suppliers, involving no risk or inventory for the customer. When cost and risk are left with a supplier, the logic is that prices will reflect the obligations the supplier has accepted and be higher than for a normal outright purchase.

Distributors

Businesses that have a large portfolio of products and a wide and diverse customer base can use distributors to manage the inventory and the high-volume, low-value transactions. This process enables a business to send whole pallets of products to a few large distributors or wholesalers, who break them down into smaller units or individual products to sell on.

This can result in substantial cost savings in handling high-volume, low-value transactions. It is the Pareto principle or the 80/20 rule, which suggests that 80% of revenue is derived from 20% of customers and vice versa. Although the percentages may not be precise, a substantial part of any organisation's infrastructure is set up to service a large group of small-value customers from whom relatively little profit is derived.

The advantage to the distributor of this approach is that it can aggregate products from a number of manufacturers and thus derive higher-value sales per customer than would be achieved from a single manufacturer.

Production

In a production process, the earlier a commitment is made to one variant of a product portfolio the higher are the levels of inventory required, because inventory of each variant needs to be kept. If the commitment is made at the point of customer order, only components need to be held. For example, a carmaker that builds cars in advance of receiving a customer order would need to pre-select attributes such as a paint colour and interior fabric. If the combination proves unpopular, the variant will remain in inventory a long time. However, if the car is painted and trimmed after an order is placed, there is no need for any finished inventory to be held and far more colour options can be offered. The disadvantage of this approach is the time delay between an order being placed and the finished product being delivered. The five types of supply model are described in Table 4.3.

By using central warehouses that frequently deliver to the outlets, much of the advantage of level 2 (fulfil and deliver from stock) can be gained by those at level 1 (fulfil and sell from stock). This enables each outlet to maintain low levels of safety inventory.

The operational advantages and disadvantages of each level are illustrated in Figure 4.9, which shows that there is no ideal position. Depending on the nature of the business and customer requirements, the optimum supply model can be identified.

Supply

This is the process described below in the order to cash cycle. Customers set up an account and place orders, goods are delivered and cash is collected. The critical factor in this process is selling only to customers that have the ability to pay.

TABLE 4.3 **Five supply models**

	Example	**Inventory issues**
Fulfil and sell from stock	Retailer with lots of outlets	Limited range. Demand in each location may not be even requiring high levels of safety stock to be held in each outlet
Fulfil and deliver from stock	An online retailer with a central distribution point	Delay in distribution and fulfilment of customer need. Demand pattern is more predictable requiring lower levels of safety stock. Greater range can be offered
Assemble to order	Computer companies with products built from subassemblies	Delay in production, though products can be tailored to customer requirements allowing a wide range of options
Make to order	Restaurant where meals are made to order from pre-purchased raw ingredients	Personalised product provision allowing wide choice and minimal finished-product waste
Source and make to order	Shipbuilder where components or raw materials are purchased after an order is received	Long time to design and source before production can be commenced. Highly individualised products

FIG 4.9 **Advantages and disadvantages of supply models**

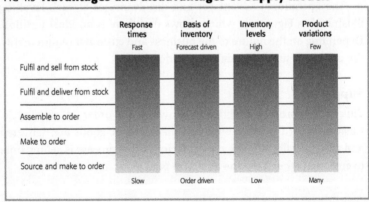

Warehousing

This is the storage of goods between their arrival and dispatch (or use in a production process). Essentially it can be regarded as waste: cash tied up that is not doing anything for the business while goods are sitting on shelves. There are some important housekeeping principles, such as knowing what is in the warehouse, where it is and how old it is so it can be accessed in the correct order and efficiently. This should extend to good practice storage to avoid damage and loss, especially of high-value items.

In essence, it is the buying and selling operations that determine inventory levels; warehouse management just provides the buffer for the inefficiencies between arrival and dispatch.

The order to cash cycle: managing receivables

The order to cash (sometimes known as O2C) or sales cycle typically involves five stages and starts with the establishment or management of a customer account. A credit limit enables customers to place orders and allows them to make payments after the delivery of their products or services. Invoices and statements specify the amounts owed and the terms for settlement.

The aim is to complete the cycle as quickly as possible and, importantly, to do so with as few errors as possible. Errors, however minor, are frequently used as excuses for halting the cycle and for customers to delay payment. The effect can be costly in both the expense involved in resolving the issue and the adverse effect on cash flow due to delayed settlement.

FIG 4.10 **The order to cash cycle**

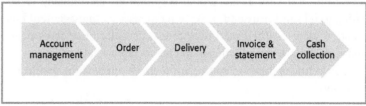

| Account management | Order | Delivery | Invoice & statement | Cash collection |

Account management

Customer accounts

A customer account specifies two things: trading terms and settlement terms. It is important to be clear about the purpose of each:

- Trading terms are about managing profitability and involve prices, discounts, overrides for achieving quantities, and so on.
- Settlement terms are about managing risk and involve the credit limit (or exposure to default), the period of credit allowed before settlement and any prompt-payment discounts.

This book is more concerned with the latter as non-payment and periods of credit have a significant impact on cash. All settlement involves the risk of bad debt from non-payment, whether through companies becoming insolvent, credit-card fraud or even forged bank notes. Taking care to check out the counterparty and the means of settlement can reduce the losses, but it will never eliminate them altogether.

It is essential to establish the right terms in the preliminary negotiations, as it will be difficult to make them more advantageous later on. As customers grow they often become more demanding and want the business to give away more in annual negotiations.

A business's credit policy provides a fundamental basis of operations and should not be arrived at by default. It should be a senior management, even a board, decision, which should determine credit criteria, the credit-rating agency to be used, the standard payment terms, the procedure for authorising any variation, the requirements for regular reporting, and so on. The policy should be written down and kept up to date, noting any changes in the creditworthiness of customers and any warnings about poor experiences. It should be disseminated to all sales staff, the financial controller and the board.

The process of setting up a customer account and establishing a credit limit will vary. Large, global corporations are unlikely to be willing to fill out forms and provide references, so management has to take a view on their creditworthiness. Smaller businesses need careful analysis, especially those that are recently established.

Typical information in setting up a credit application would be as follows:

- Name, address, phone number, e-mail address, website.
- Type of business and trade – company, partnership, sole trader, non-profit, etc.
- Credit limit requested and settlement method.
- Credit check by a credit-rating agency such as Dun & Bradstreet.
- Bank reference (including the nature of collateral the bank holds against default).
- Trade references (2–4 other suppliers and the length of relationship). Bear in mind these are likely to be their best references and thus they will not necessarily be indicative of how they deal with all their suppliers. An interesting question (which is unlikely to be answered accurately) is why they left their previous supplier.
- Copies of last three years' annual accounts on which performance and ratio analysis can be completed.
- For start-up businesses without a track record, any personal guarantee that can be provided by the owner(s).
- For new businesses or sole traders, some proof of identity: a copy of a certificate of incorporation or bank statements to provide evidence that the business and its owners are genuine.

A credit check completed by one of the credit-rating agencies will take into account factors such as:

- evidence of a sustainable and profitable business;
- leverage of under 50% (see Chapter 3);
- track record of payment history;
- tangible net worth – the surplus uncharged assets available to creditors;
- the relative performance of the business compared to others in its industry sector;
- details of court judgments against the business;
- details of existing mortgages and charges taken by lenders over assets;
- details of directors and their other directorships.

Using this information the agency will provide its assessment of a potential customer's financial strength, risk and maximum credit limit. The same analysis should be completed as part of an account review to identify any credit deterioration. It must be noted that the analysis based on published accounts will only ever be historic and potentially a year or more out of date. Examining recent payment history and watching for signals such as reduced orders and late payment are likely to be much better early warnings that a customer's business situation has changed. However, as John Argenti, founder of the Strategic Planning Society, said:

> Failure cannot be forecasted by merely looking at signs of financial deterioration. This deterioration only occurs towards the end of the process of failure. It is better to look at where the process starts, which is almost certainly not financial, it is managerial and it can be seen long before the company's financial position begins to deteriorate.

Supplying the information for a credit application is an onerous obligation for potential customers and may become a barrier to securing their business, particularly if competitors' requirements are less demanding. Thus the creation of a credit account becomes a matter of judgment: how much risk is involved versus the resources required to mitigate that risk. In many organisations a points system is used where each completed item on the list earns points (references being scored higher that other items). Various total scores are required depending on the size of the credit limit. For example:

- If the credit limit is less than 1% of annual revenue, 10 points are needed.
- If the credit limit is greater than 1% but less than 5% of annual revenue, 15 points are needed.
- If the credit limit is greater than 5% of annual revenue, 25 points are needed.

The points required are also reduced or increased depending on how significant the credit limit is to the customer. While the amount of credit may be less than 1% for the supply business, it may be 30%

of purchases for a customer that is a much smaller business. If the latter were to get into trouble, there would be a higher likelihood of loss than if the credit limit were restricted to 1% of the customer's business. In these circumstances extra credit-scoring points would be needed.

The credit limit should not need to be more than the amount required to purchase two months' worth of supplies, as payment should be received within 60 days allowing continual trade. For a growing business this may need to increase to allow up to 90 days of purchases. For initial transactions after setting up an account a lower limit may be preferable, with a review and an increase in limit after 3–6 months of successful trade and prompt payment.

Where a credit limit cannot be justified because of a customer's poor credit reference or because it is a new business that has no history on which to base a judgment, trade can still be done either by cash in advance or by use of a bank guarantee, where the customer's bank will take the credit risk (see letters of credit below).

Terms and conditions

Once an account has been set up the customer should be given a copy of the payment terms and conditions before an order is accepted. The customer should sign this as evidence of agreement, which is a useful reference if there are delays in payment that breach the terms and conditions.

A typical document should include:

- product prices;
- delivery arrangements;
- credit limit;
- payment terms;
- the right to charge interest on late payments and claim compensation for debt recovery costs;
- retention of title (the supplier retains ownership of the goods supplied until they are paid for);
- time limits for raising a dispute;
- circumstances in which a contract might be breached.

The credit terms that a business offers can be an intrinsic part of the overall customer proposition – for example, a furniture company that offers interest-free credit for a year, or a car company that extends credit over three years. These terms aid sales but have both a cost and a cash flow effect which the business will need to fund (see also vendor finance programmes below). Accelerating cash collection may not always be best for the overall business model.

Foreign exchange

Where supply is derived in one currency and settlement is in another, it is important to be clear about the currency used for transactions and who will bear any foreign-exchange gains or losses. For volatile currencies, movements in exchange rates over a two-month settlement period can double or eliminate any profit on the transaction. To minimise the risk it may be worth hedging the exchange rates (see Chapter 3) or having accelerated payments.

Order

Purchase orders

Many companies have a purchase-order system through which all orders must be placed. A purchase-order number is the authority to buy and the key to being paid; without it invoices will be rejected. So before accepting an order to supply, it is necessary to understand how your customer's purchasing system works, including the ordering, the goods receipt and the invoice-handling systems. Understanding and following correct procedures will ensure that paperwork is not rejected and payment is made on time. Documenting the process, the names of the people involved and your experience of the system is effective in helping ensure future transactions benefit from the knowledge acquired.

Before an order is processed it is therefore necessary to comply with the customer's system and have the requisite purchase-order numbers and paperwork in place. Quick fixes and a "we'll do that later" attitude inevitably result in invoice rejection and protracted settlement. If a customer does not issue purchase orders, it can be helpful to send a confirmation by post or e-mail as a means of documenting what has been agreed. This is particularly relevant for telephone orders where the authority of the person placing the order cannot be easily validated.

Vendor finance

Where extended credit terms are offered to customers as part of the deal, such as for expensive cars or furniture, it is common to have low-interest or even interest-free finance available to facilitate the purchase. Businesses offering these deals may not want to carry the cost of funding this credit or accept the repayment risk, so they set up a vendor finance programme with a bank that takes on the debt and collects it in the same way as it would a normal loan. The incentive for the bank is that it pays the retailer less than the amount it collects from the customer. For example, if a piece of furniture is on sale for $1,000 with interest-free credit, the bank gives the retailer, say, $900 and takes the difference of $100 to cover the cost of interest until cash is received from the customer. These finance packages are often branded, so the customer receives retailer-branded communications and does not know about the financial institution behind the transaction.

The bank that is financing the transaction will require a credit check on the customer, so delivery of the goods cannot go ahead until the bank has given its approval.

Letters of credit

When businesses trade across country borders collecting cash becomes more difficult. There are potentially two legal systems operating and pursuing the customer can be expensive. A letter of credit or documentary credit (DC) can be used to provide a payment contract for goods or services. This is an irrevocable payment obligation drawn up by the customer's bank that binds the bank to pay a fixed sum of money to another party on fulfilment of certain criteria (the delivery of goods). The credit risk is therefore with the customer's bank and not the customer itself.

The process, which is illustrated in Figure 4.11, is as follows:

FIG 4.11 **Letter of credit process**

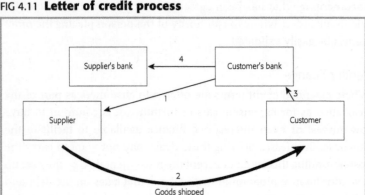

1. A customer asks a bank to raise a letter of credit, which is sent to the supplier guaranteeing payment in exchange for the delivery of goods and the supply of suitable documentation as evidence of contract fulfilment.

2. The goods are shipped.

3. The bank is advised that the contract terms have been fulfilled.

4. The customer's bank pays the supplier's bank.

There are also standby letters of credit (or bank guarantees). These are issued by banks to confirm that a customer has the ability to pay and meet the terms of a contract. The credit risk is primarily with the customer, and only if the terms of the standby letter of credit are not complied with will the bank be required to honour the guarantee.

Export credit guarantees

Governments are generally keen to promote exports and often support international trade. Some operate export credit guarantee schemes that operate much like insurance. For a small payment a debt can be guaranteed, and on various conditions an export credit agency will pay the debt and assume responsibility for its collection, thus avoiding the need for a letter of credit.

Delivery

The delivery stage may seem a simple part of the process, but it is essential to have documented evidence to show that title to any goods has been handed over to the customer. Without evidence a customer can deny receipt and thus refuse payment. The difficulty arises when there is no one available to formally receive the goods. At the order stage it is important to agree not only where and when the products are to be delivered, but also how they will be signed for.

Any paperwork should itemise the goods being delivered. For small orders, the customer can check the goods before the delivery note is signed. For larger orders, it may have to be signed as a palette or box count. Disputes can arise over damaged or missing items, so any visual damage (even to packaging) should be specified on the delivery note. With the advent of cheap digital cameras, a photograph of the goods also provides evidence, especially for high-value items, in particular their condition on arrival.

Invoice and statement

Invoicing is normally done once the goods or services have been delivered. The invoice should be issued as soon as possible and not left until the end of the month. The quicker it is approved and entered on the customer's system the sooner payment will be received.

The easiest way for a customer to delay payment is to find an error in an invoice, be slow to advise the supplier of the error, and be slow to accept the revisions. Consequently, it is worth taking time to get the invoice right in the first place. This includes matching the details to the purchase order – specifically quantities, prices, discounts – and quoting the purchase-order number as a reference.

Any required corrections should be made promptly and quickly followed up to ensure the matter has been resolved to the customer's satisfaction. The longer an invoice sits unapproved the longer it will be before payment is secured. It may also be worth recording the cause of the dispute so that it can be investigated, and also to prevent repetition on the same or other accounts.

A statement is a summary of all invoices, receipts and any

credit notes (for returns) over, generally, a month, giving a total of the amount outstanding. A statement is a means of confirming all the transactions in that month, and often provides the prompt for payment 30 days later.

Cash collection

Collecting cash is rarely easy, but it is made easier by building a relationship with customers rather than treating it as a routine task. If a business has a good relationship with its customers, they are more likely to have an eye on business continuity and treat it respectfully.

The process hinges on the careful monitoring of aged invoices and accounts that are near their credit limit. High-value accounts should be prioritised and the collection process should be spread over several stages. It is worth remembering that there is a balance between the need to extract payment for one or two late invoices and maintaining a relationship with a customer who may continue to purchase from you for a long time. It is also worth bearing in mind that a pre-emptive call can be more helpful to advise that an account is about to be overdue or that a limit has been reached than a reactive one when the breach of terms has occurred.

The stages in the collection process are as follows:

- Telephone contact to ask when an overdue payment can be expected. All such calls should be logged, recording time, date, the name of the person spoken to and the reply given. Where appropriate a written record of the call should be sent to the customer confirming what has been agreed.

- Put the account on stop. A period of grace is often given, but at some stage it may become necessary to consider whether the account will be put on stop until payment has been received. The threat will often trigger the intended response as the customer will not want the business to be disrupted – and it protects the supplier from any further losses should the customer not pay. Everything should be put in writing even if the initial communication was by telephone.

- Threaten legal action. After attempts to extract payment have been exhausted, the next stage is to advise that legal action will commence. In such a letter the supplier should:
  - express disappointment that promises have been broken (cite the telephone conversations and letters to date);
  - note the terms and conditions that were advised when the account was set up;
  - offer a specific period for settlement, such as seven days;
  - explain clearly what will happen after this period.

If the threat of legal action does not work, the choice is to:

- follow up the threat and involve lawyers;
- potentially write off the debt on the grounds that what is spent on lawyers and legal costs will be more than that likely to be recovered from the customer.

In most cases, encouraging customers to pay something is better than getting no payment at all. A piecemeal process or an agreed schedule of payments enables further supplies to be delivered on each receipt and thus continuity of a customer's business. It is the success of customers' future sales that will allow full repayment of debts; starving them of supplies will only make their future more uncertain.

When customers do not pay after repeated requests, it is likely that they are in significant trouble. Should a customer go bust, the official receiver will notify suppliers whether a meeting of creditors is to be held. If the customer holds significant assets, the meeting will decide how they can be released to creditors and may declare a dividend rate (such as 10 cents for every dollar owed to an unsecured creditor). There will also be a report detailing the insolvent company's assets and the reasons for its failure. For many suppliers, the liquidation of a customer often means that they have to write off any balance outstanding. The remaining assets in the business are normally insufficient to repay the preferential creditors (such as the banks), let alone provide a surplus to pay the unsecured creditors.

Automated cash collection

In many business-to-consumer companies the simplest way to collect a large number of low-value regular amounts is through automated systems such as direct debit or standing order. The money is automatically transferred on due dates, saving considerable effort in invoicing, collecting and chasing, and only unpaid collections need to be followed up. As cash arrives on the due date, it is highly predictable for forecasting purposes. Many utility, insurance and credit companies use this method. Its efficiency means that businesses are able to offer discounts to consumers who enter into these arrangements.

Late-payment interest

Under the terms and conditions of payment it is appropriate to include a provision for charging late-payment interest. The terms will identify the date from which such interest will be chargeable and the rate to be applied (normally a premium over a bank base rate). In practice, interest is rarely levied and even more rarely paid.

Helping customers through tough times

Just as a business tries to optimise its cash flow, its customers try to optimise theirs. This means that if a customer is struggling through a market downturn its cash flow will be strained and therefore a relaxation of credit terms may be in both parties' interests in order to allow trade to continue, if the belief is that the longer-term prospects are good.

The matters to consider are:

- the importance of the customer to the supplier – for a significant customer it is in the supplier's interest to develop a long-term solution to enable trade to continue;
- the importance of the supplier to the customer – where the supplier is a significant one;
- the amount involved;
- the public (and other customer) relations implications.

Credit insurance

Credit insurance can be used to insure against bad debt, within given credit limits. This offers a solution if late payments or customer insolvency could seriously harm the business. Policyholders are not fully protected against bad debt, as insurance will typically cover only 75–95% of any loss. Before providing cover, an insurer will need evidence of efficient standards of credit control and will set a credit limit based on previous sales and bad debts. The insurance comes at a price and thus the benefit versus the cost has to be weighed up.

Converting receivables into cash immediately

For a new or small business, where cash flow may be tight and administrative resources scarce, it is possible to convert receivables into cash immediately. This is achieved by letting another business take responsibility for collection. Two common methods are factoring and securitisation.

Factoring (sometimes called invoice discounting) is where a financial institution buys receivables for a discount and then takes over their collection. All factoring contracts have the following elements in common:

- Advance rate – the percentage of the accounts receivable that will be paid upfront. Some factoring companies advance the full 100%; others advance 70% and pay the balance once the receivables are collected. The typical range is 70–90% of the accounts receivable.
- Discount rate – the rate charged by the factoring company for the financing, which is effectively the interest rate on the advanced funds plus an administration fee. The typical range is 1–7% of the accounts receivable, depending on the payment terms.
- Recourse or non-recourse. In a non-recourse agreement, the factoring company bears the burden of collecting the accounts receivable. In a recourse agreement, in which the interest rates charged will be lower, the business bears the burden of bad debts (in other words, if they are uncollectable, they will be charged back).

The terms and rates will depend upon the creditworthiness of the business. Those with a few strong customers get better rates than those with lots of weak customers. Factoring is just another form of financing, so if accounts receivable are easily and simply managed it may be cheaper to borrow money.

Factoring is increasingly used for international invoice settlement, where the factoring company can provide assistance in explaining local laws, language translation, understanding local taxation and assessing the creditworthiness of potential customers. Such a combination of services can otherwise be difficult to obtain.

Securitisation is when the book receivables are sold into a shell (or new) company and investors seeking a short-term investment hope to make an appropriate return for the risk in collection. This type of transaction is appropriate only for large amounts. For example, mobile telephone companies used it to accelerate cash receipts while they were building their networks. Small mortgage companies, whose size prevents them taking on too much debt, also use it – they build a mortgage book and periodically sell it off to fund the building of the next book.

In both types of transaction the counterparties are seeking to make a profit. If a business decides to use this approach, it should be a result of careful cash flow planning, knowing the expected gearing position and anticipated WACC percentage (see Chapter 3) to determine the most cost-effective way of financing its operations.

Discounts for early payment

It may seem a good idea to offer an incentive such as a discount for prompt payment. However, the discount needs to be at a substantially better rate than the marginal rate at which the customer would be borrowing money. This makes it expensive, as there is a direct loss of profit on each transaction. It can also be unproductive, as some customers will just take the discount and still pay late, thus reducing profitability without the cash flow benefit. A period of flexibility should be allowed – perhaps up to five days late – after which the discount should be removed, and if abused it should be withdrawn from future invoices.

Table 4.4 shows the cost of a customer paying late. The top row is the WACC in the business (see Chapter 3), and the first column shows the number of days of credit. Offering a discount lower than the rate quoted will be advantageous to the business, but it may not be sufficient to encourage a customer to change its settlement arrangements.

TABLE 4.4 **The cost of late payment**

Cost of capital (WACC), %							
	8	**9**	**10**	**11**	**12**	**13**	**14**
Days of credit							
30	0.66	0.74	0.82	0.90	0.99	1.07	1.15
40	0.88	0.99	1.10	1.21	1.32	1.42	1.53
50	1.10	1.23	1.37	1.51	1.64	1.78	1.92
60	1.32	1.48	1.64	1.81	1.97	2.14	2.30
70	1.53	1.73	1.92	2.11	2.30	2.49	2.68
80	1.75	1.97	2.19	2.41	2.63	2.85	3.07

Physical cash handling

In almost all business-to-business and an increasing proportion of business-to-consumer transactions settlement is made by electronic, card or paper (cheques) transfer. Only in low-value settlements, typically in retailing, is cash used. As cash is so desirable and easy to hide there is a high propensity for theft unless tight controls are imposed to minimise opportunities and catch miscreants. Also the cost of moving cash can be high, especially if a third party is required to transport the cash from the business to the bank.

There are four things businesses can do to help manage the risk of holding cash from the time it is received through to when it is lodged at the bank:

■ Recruitment. Ensure that appropriate references are taken and checks are made on staff who will be in contact with cash.

■ Separation of duties. Separate people should be responsible for receiving cash, counting cash, making bank deposits and reconciling lodgements to point-of-sale (cash) registers. Where possible two or more people should be present for cash movements.

■ Secure vaults. Cash should be stored during the day and overnight in secure vaults that are time locked. The float kept at the point of sale should be only enough to provide change. As cash builds up during the day it should be securely stored; floor vaults under the point-of-sale registers can be used for this purpose.

■ Cash counts. Regularly count the cash in point-of-sale registers and reconcile this with the sales listing. Preferably this should be done at the end of each shift or at each change of staff member.

Video surveillance of point-of-sale registers and vaults can be a deterrent as well as a means of identifying any culprits.

Beyond cash

There is an expectation that some time in the future cash will cease to be in physical form. Contactless smartcards (such as those used in the UK on London's transport system) and mobile money (used in Africa to send money by text message) will become the main ways to transact. Already there are twice as many mobile phones in the world as bank accounts. At present these cashless payment methods are limited and often restricted to micro-payments as they do not involve authentication.

There is also talk of a more sophisticated cashless society, with microchips implanted in our hands and mobile-phone invoices becoming bank statements. Willingness to embrace these innovations should provide for businesses greater security of receipt, and for governments a more auditable set of transactions for tax-levying purposes and prevention of money-laundering.

5 Investment opportunities

THE INVESTMENT OF CASH involves selecting the right assets at the right time at the right price. The purchases, be they property, equipment or another business, will be among the largest a business makes. Thus a legacy of poor investment selection can be a burden for many years, with the interest and capital repayments on the debt to fund them being a substantial drain on cash.

It is therefore paramount that there is a credible evaluation of the potential returns from an investment before the terms on which the investment is made are agreed and cash is committed. After all, the ability to exit a lease or sell an asset can be limited (particularly in the case of a bespoke or specialist asset).

The means of purchase of an asset is an important consideration: should it be purchased outright or perhaps leased or rented? Each method brings different risks, rewards and effects on cash flow; there is no best way to acquire the use of an asset.

This chapter explores three aspects:

- Techniques to forecast the financial benefits that are expected to be derived from acquiring an asset.
- Methods of determining whether the forecast financial benefits justify the investment.
- Selection of the appropriate means of acquiring the asset.

Many businesses use a business case to document and evaluate the potential of an investment opportunity. This typically consists of background information on the strategic benefit and operational need, a cash flow forecast of likely receipts and payments, an evaluation of the cash flow forecast and an explanation of risks. The business case forms the basis of a review and approval process involving various senior individuals and potentially the board. For a detailed explanation see *The Economist Guide to Financial Management* by John Tennent.

The financial case for investment

The first stage in evaluating the financial case for investment is to create a robust model of the forecast operational cash flows. These are normally split into three categories:

- Capex, short for capital expenditure, which is the purchase of balance-sheet items, such as fixed assets.
- Revenue, the cash receipts from the sale of products or services.
- Opex, short for operating expenditure, which includes items typically found on an income statement such as payroll or utilities.

Table 5.1 shows a cash flow analysis for a small manufacturing business. A machine is purchased for $1,000 at the outset. Revenue starts being earned and grows as the product is marketed. The opex costs are a combination of fixed costs (salaries) and variable costs (raw materials). Overall, the net cash flow received or paid each year is what is required to go on and value the investment opportunity.

TABLE 5.1 **A cash flow analysis**

	0	1	2	3	4	5
Capex	(1,000)					
Revenue		100	300	700	1,200	1,500
Opex		(210)	(240)	(300)	(390)	(430)
Net cash flow	(1,000)	(110)	60	400	810	1,070

The cash flows are just the future receipts and payments; any costs that have already been paid, such as for research, are excluded as they have already been sunk into the project. Regardless of the approval outcome, these costs cannot be recovered.

At this stage all funding cash flows such as debt, equity, interest and dividends should be excluded, as the purpose of the evaluation is to determine whether the operating cash flows generate an attractive enough return to warrant committing investment.

If the annual net cash flows are accumulated, the profile of overall cash investment is revealed (see Table 5.2).

TABLE 5.2 **Accumulated net cash flow**

	0	1	2	3	4	5
Net cash flow	(1,000)	(110)	60	400	810	1,070
Cumulative cash flow	(1,000)	(1,110)	(1,050)	(650)	160	1,230

A typical cumulative cash flow profile over the life of a project can be represented by graph that is known as a J curve (see Figure 5.1).

At the outset money is spent and this takes the cash flow into deficit. As receipts increase and the payments decrease, the bottom of the trough is reached. The increasing receipts eventually turn the cumulative cash flow positive and the project starts to yield the benefits of the investment. However, these benefits may not be sustainable owing to competitive pressures or technology changes, and the cash flows may plateau or even fall.

FIG 5.1 **A J curve**

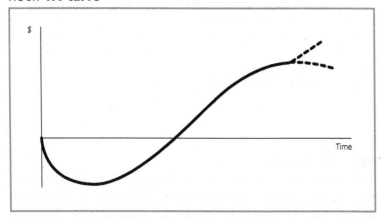

The impact on cash flow is that the trough (the area below the time axis) will be a period of funding requirement and the surplus (the area above the time axis) will be a period of cash surplus. In building the cash flow forecasts for the business (as shown in Chapter 2), the effects of new investments, such as the one illustrated above, should be included.

Assembling a cash flow forecast
Cash flow

The analysis is based exclusively on cash flows rather than profit flows. Cash flows include the receipts and payments for a project's revenues, costs, capital expenditure and taxation. The first step is to distinguish between profit flows and cash flows. Some of the principal differences are explained in Chapter 1 and summarised in Table 5.3.

TABLE 5.3 **Differences between profit flow and cash flow**

Type of data	Profit flow	Cash flow
Revenue	Recognised when the product or service is delivered	Recognised when the receivable is paid
Cost of sales	Recognised when the product or service is delivered (held as inventory until this point)	Recognised when cash is paid out to suppliers and the items are taken into inventory
Overheads	Spread evenly over the period of benefit using the concepts of accruals and prepayments	Recognised when the cash is paid for each item (typically in arrears)
Taxation	Based on profits earned in a year	Typically paid by instalments or in the year after it has been earned
Fixed assets	The cost is spread over the period of use through depreciation	Recognised in total at the time of purchase (unless paid by instalments)

Relevant revenues

Only incremental revenues that are generated as a direct result of the business decision should be included. Existing or anticipated revenue streams resulting from earlier decisions should be excluded.

Incremental revenues may be the result of events such as the launch of a new product or service or a successful advertising campaign. If the launch of a new product or service is likely to reduce sales of an existing product or service, this should be shown as lost revenue as a consequence of the investment.

Relevant costs and capital expenditure

Relevant costs and items of capital expenditure are those that would arise solely as a result of the proposed project. Any costs or capital expenditure that are subject to pre-existing, legally binding contracts should be excluded. The costs and capital expenditure must also be cash items. Any items that do not include incremental cash should be excluded, so depreciation charges, notional rents and internal cross charges should all be excluded from the appraisal.

Relevant taxes

Businesses pay income or corporation tax on their profits and this represents a cash cost to the business. However, tax is calculated after the charging of interest, and as finance charges are not relevant costs the corporation tax paid must be calculated as if the business paid no interest.

Cash flow examples

The main types of cash flow to include and exclude are shown in Table 5.4.

TABLE 5.4 **Cash flows to include and exclude**

Cash flows to include	Cash flows to exclude
Cash generated from revenue	Equity or loan finance (received or repaid)
Cash paid for purchases	Dividend or interest on the finance
Cash paid for running costs	Lease payments[a]
Cash paid and received on the purchase or sale of assets	Interest received on surplus deposits
The equivalent cash purchase cost for assets that would otherwise have been leased[a]	
Tax payments or receipts	

a Assets that are leased have a special treatment in the cash flows.

Essentially there are two types of lease (see later in this chapter) and each has its own treatment:

■ Operating leases are usually short term, for example rent, and are treated in the same way as other opex costs.

■ Finance leases typically span the life of the asset and are similar to purchasing by instalments. The lease payments are calculated to include not just the cost of the asset but also the interest on funding the lessor's investment in the asset. As cash flow models should exclude funding costs, the asset subject to a finance lease should be shown as an equivalent purchase cost at the point of first use. The equivalent purchase cost can be found by discounting the lease payments at the implicit rate of interest in the transaction (see discounting below).

The cash effect of change

It can be difficult to know where to start when building the cash flows for a project. For example, a business may want to assess the impact on manufacturing costs of introducing new product packaging. An accurate and perhaps time-consuming way would be to evaluate the current packaging cost and the new packaging cost and compare the results. A more efficient way would be to evaluate the effect of changing from the current situation to the new situation. This can be done by assuming that production with the old packaging will continue and then identifying any receipts and payments that will be different when switching to the new packaging.

The benefits of this approach are that there is only one cash flow analysis and that it focuses exclusively on those aspects of manufacturing that will be affected by the change. Anything that is unaffected by the change is ignored. This approach can be applied to an acquisition, a product launch, a closure or any capital expenditure. The important point is to focus on the cash effect of the changes that will take place as a consequence of a decision to go ahead.

Dealing with allocated overheads

In compiling the cash flows, there can be a conflict between assessing the project on its own and assessing it as part of the business. In Table 5.4, cash paid for running costs can incorporate central overheads that are allocated to a product or department.

An example is a new product launch in a factory that already makes several other products. The cost of the factory (rent, heat, light and canteen) is allocated to products on a dollar per tonne basis. On the launch of this new product the organisation is unlikely to be spending much more on the factory, yet part of the cost can now be attributed to the new product.

If the factory cost is ignored in the analysis of the new product, the financial evaluation will show unrealistically low manufacturing costs. The implication could be that the new product will be viable only if the other products in the factory are able to cover the factory costs. This is the principle (and danger) of marginal costing. To deal with this problem, some companies have developed a principle that they apply to all projects: treat the project as part of the company and develop the cash flows for overheads as follows:

- If the project is to add business to the company, assume its share of allocated overheads is a real cash flow cost, typically charged on a revenue or unit basis, and thus include this in the cash flow analysis of the project.

- If the project is to remove business from the company, assume there will be no cash flow saving in the total company overheads and thus exclude any overhead items from the project evaluation.

This principle is perhaps prudent in the impact it can have on projects and may be seen as negating the economy of scale effect. In any proposal it is worth stating clearly the way overheads have been treated. Some businesses require financial analysis of new product proposals to be calculated twice – once including allocated overheads and once excluding them – in order to get a better understanding of the project.

Sign convention

In building the cash flow forecasts the standard convention is that a cash receipt is positive and a cash payment is negative.

Cash flow timing

Most project cash flows are forecast with annual time intervals. The standard layout is shown in Figure 5.2.

Time 0 is the moment the first cash flow takes place. Time 1 is one year after the first cash flow takes place, time 2 is two years after the first cash flow takes place, and so on. Under these assumptions, all cash inflows and outflows during any particular year are assumed to take place at either the beginning or the end of the year. With these annual intervals it can be difficult to identify the appropriate point at which to place a cash flow. An overriding principle is to be prudent and if necessary accelerate payments and defer receipts. The following general rules apply:

- Capex outflows should be placed at the start of a year. With a large capital spend they may be spread over the first few years of the project and thus the expenditure in any year would be put at the start of that year.

- Revenue is typically shown at the end of the year in which it has been received.

- Opex costs are normally shown as being matched against the revenue they supported. Caution would suggest they should be shown at the beginning of the year in which they are paid, but

FIG 5.2 **Cash flow time intervals**

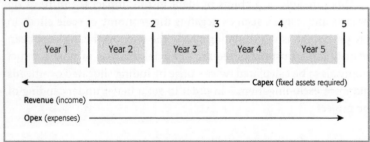

the principle of matching overrules. Thus the cash profit in any year is deferred to the end of the year in which it is earned.

The effect of these prudent timings is to make the project appear slightly less financially attractive than it really is.

Time periods

There are two dimensions to time periods:

- How far into the future should be predicted?
- What unit of time should be used – years, quarters or months?

There are no general rules, but working on the basis that it is easier to predict next year than it is to predict ten years ahead, if the cash flows arising more than a decade ahead are critical to the success or failure of a project, it is a high-risk project. Even dependency beyond five years can be risky.

For many proposals the nature of the project will determine the duration of evaluation. For example:

- Advertising campaigns or promotions – up to three months by week.
- IT projects – up to four years by quarter.
- Manufacturing – up to ten years by year.
- Buildings or construction – up to 20 years by year.

The length of time over which projections are made is based on the potential life cycle of the product. Other factors such as fade and competition will cause margins to erode over time. Thus future years may have the benefit of higher volumes but at potentially lower margins. For electronic products the impact of destructive technology can also play a part. Destructive technologies are innovations – such as digital music downloads – that damage or destroy others. It is unrealistic to make long-term production projections for products susceptible to such a threat.

Residual values

For capital expenditure it is often relatively easy to identify the upfront purchase or construction costs. It is more difficult to identify the end cash flows such as disposal proceeds or costs. For example, a proposal for a nuclear power station could include designs and tenders and therefore accurately identify construction cost. At the end of its useful life in 30 years' time the unknowns are how much the site will be worth and how much should be allowed for decommissioning and decontamination.

Some general principles are as follows:

■ **Cars.** In evaluating car ownership it is reasonable to assume a resale value using guides to second-hand value. Such guides indicate that after four years a car is worth about 25% of purchase cost.

■ **Plant.** Most companies do not buy equipment and machinery with an intention of resale. This is partly because there is a limited second-hand market and partly because technology changes cause obsolescence (for example computers). In such cases no residual value should be assumed, apart from scrap values for materials.

■ **Buildings.** For special purpose buildings it would be prudent to assume no residual value. For office buildings that have alternative uses a residual value is appropriate depending upon location.

■ **Land.** In evaluating the residual value of land there are four main considerations:
  - Will the activity on the land contaminate or change its value (eg, a chemical storage facility)?
  - Is the value affected by factors that may be subject to change (eg, a retail site that is reliant on passing trade that would decline should a bypass be built)?
  - Can the land be used for another purpose (eg, housing)?
  - How will inflation and market conditions change its value (eg, will it hold or gain value with time)?

As well as identifying residual values and costs, it is helpful to identify exit costs during the life of the project. Should a 25-year project not deliver the desired benefits, it would be useful to know the cost of exit after 5, 10, 15 and 20 years.

The effects of working capital

Working capital consists of inventory, receivables and payables (as explained in Chapter 4). These are the items in the balance sheet that tie up cash, but normally turn over quite quickly. Their effect on cash flows is normally a timing delay of a month or two; for example, if customers normally pay their invoices within a month of receipt, then any sales made in December will not turn into cash until January.

TABLE 5.5 **The effect of timing delays on cash from receivables**

Year	Revenue	Cash calculation	Total cash received	Receivables
1	1,200	1,200 × 11/12 = 1100	1,100	100
2	2,400	1,200 × 1/12 = 100		
		2,400 × 11/12 = 2200	2,300	200
3	3,600	2,400 × 1/12 = 200		
		3,600 × 11/12 = 3300	3,500	300
4	0	3,600 × 1/12 = 300	300	0
Total	7,200		7,200	

Table 5.6 illustrates the way this is often shown in cash flows.

TABLE 5.6 **Timing delays in cash from receivables**

Year	Revenue	Net receivables	Net cash
1	1,200	(100)	1,100
2	2,400	(100)	2,300
3	3,600	(100)	3,500
4	0	300	300
Total	7,200	0	7,200

The effect of receivables is not to lose money but to delay its receipt. Although in cash flows it is wrong to assume that working capital is never lost, as there will or may be bad debts.

Similar effects arise for payables where cash payments lag behind the receipt of inventory and consumables. For inventory a base quantity needs to be held, so this can be shown as an investment arriving at time 0 and being released at the end of the project.

For foreign trade settlement times can lengthen; and bank charges and exchange rates may mean that less cash is received than the sum invoiced (as explained in Chapter 3).

Valuation of the cash flow forecast

Once the cash flow projections for an investment have been identified, the next stage is to complete a quantitative appraisal of those cash flows as a basis for deciding whether the anticipated benefits are sufficient compensation for the risk involved.

The quantitative appraisal techniques are:

■ payback;
■ net present value (NPV);
■ internal rate of return (IRR) and modified internal rate of return (MIRR).

In Table 5.7, two projects are used to illustrate the techniques. Both involve an investment of $10,000 now, but each has a different profile of cash returns over its five-year life.

TABLE 5.7 **Cash returns from projects**

| | Project A | | Project B | |
	Cash out	Cash in	Cash out	Cash in
Year 0	(10,000)		(10,000)	
Year 1		1,000		5,000
Year 2		2,000		4,000
Year 3		3,000		3,000
Year 4		4,000		2,000
Year 5		5,000		
Total	(10,000)	15,000	(10,000)	14,000

At first glance project A appears to be the better option. Over the five years it achieves a surplus of $5,000 over the money invested whereas project B achieves only $4,000. However, project B returns the money faster, and getting the return earlier will reduce the risk in the investment. The quantitative techniques help evaluate the risk and reward in the project to determine which would be preferable.

Payback

This is the simplest method of investment appraisal. It provides a quantification of risk in terms of measuring how quickly the original investment is returned. The general principle is that projects which recoup their initial cash investment faster are more attractive. Risk here is defined as uncertainty, because predicting cash flows next year is likely to be more accurate than predicting those in five years' time. The measure is the time taken to reach the cash break-even point, when the total cash out equals the total cash in.

On the cumulative cash flow curve, the payback is the time it takes for the line to return to zero (see Figure 5.3).

Table 5.8 shows the effect of payback in projects A and B.

TABLE 5.8 **Calculating payback**

| | Project A | | Project B | |
	Cash movements	**Net investment**	**Cash movements**	**Net investment**
Year 0	(10,000)	(10,000)	(10,000)	(10,000)
Year 1	1,000	(9,000)	5,000	(5,000)
Year 2	2,000	(7,000)	4,000	(1,000)
Year 3	3,000	(4,000)	3,000	2,000
Year 4	4,000	0	2,000	4,000
Year 5	5,000	5,000		
Total	5,000		4,000	

The payback for project A is four years and for project B is two years and four months (if cash is earned evenly through each year). Many companies use this measure to reject projects that do not pay

FIG 5.3 **Payback**

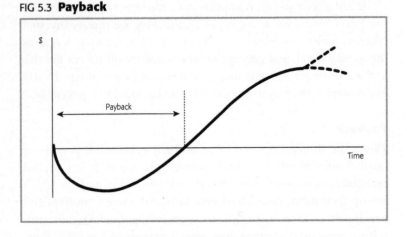

back within a set period. If a project has a payback of over ten years, only governments and large corporations are likely to accept the risk and back it.

The problem with payback is that it is a short-term measure. It fails to consider cash flows beyond the payback period (for example, project A could make $2m in year 6 and its payback would still be four years). It also makes no allowance for interest and therefore does not measure the return made by a project.

Net present value

This method shows the surplus cash made by an investment after funding costs have been deducted. It uses the principle of discounting cash flows. For example, if someone is offered $100 now or $100 in one year's time, they will choose to receive $100 today, because if interest rates are 10% and the $100 is invested, in one year it will have grown to $110. This is the concept of the time value of money. The future value of $100 at a 10% interest rate is shown in Table 5.9.

TABLE 5.9 **The future value of $100 at 10% interest rates**

Now	In 1 year	In 2 years	In 3 years	In 4 years	In 5 years
$100	$110.00	$121.00	$133.10	$146.41	$161.051

FIG 5.4 **Net present value**

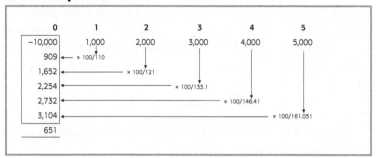

This uses the principle of compound interest. However, if someone is offered $110 in one year's time or $121 in two years' time with interest rates still at 10%, the choice becomes more difficult. From Table 5.9 it is clear that they are both worth $121 at the end of two years. The ability to compare depends on choosing the same point in time whether it is now, in two years' time or in ten years' time. Each cash flow needs to be either compounded to find a future value or discounted to find a present value.

The two options would both be the equivalent of receiving $100 today. The principle of working out what a future cash flow is worth now is the basis for all project appraisal and company valuations. The year 0 (now) value of a future cash flow is known as its present value (PV). Adding together the PV of each cash flow in a project provides the net present value (NPV).

To find the NPV of the cash flows in project A the procedure is as follows: using a discount rate of 10%, each future cash flow can be multiplied by 100 and divided by the compound interest value from Table 5.9 (see Figure 5.4).

The NPV of project A is therefore $651, which is substantially less than the apparent surplus of $5,000 found by simply adding the series of cash flows. The reduction is caused by having to fund the investment in the early years of the project.

A better way to find the PV of a cash flow is to use the formula:

$$\text{Future value} \times \frac{1}{(1 + \text{interest rate}) \, \char94 \, \text{number of years}} = \text{present value}$$

To apply the formula the interest rate is expressed as a fraction so 10% would be shown as 0.1. The ^ symbol means to the power; for example, if the number of years is two, the denominator is squared.

The present value of $2,000 received in two years' time when interest rates are 10% is:

$$2,000 \times \frac{1}{(1 + 0.1)\,^\wedge\,2} = 1,652$$

Expressed another way, if $1,652 is put on deposit today at 10%, it will be worth $2,000 after two years.

Applying this formula to projects A and B will have the effect shown in Table 5.10, assuming the cost of money is 10%.

TABLE 5.10 **Net present value calculations**

		10% discount factor	Present value
Project A			
Year 0	(10,000)	1.0000	(10,000)
Year 1	1,000	0.9091	909
Year 2	2,000	0.8264	1,652
Year 3	3,000	0.7513	2,254
Year 4	4,000	0.6830	2,732
Year 5	5,000	0.6209	3,104
Net present value			651
Project B			
Year 0	(10,000)	1.0000	(10,000)
Year 1	5,000	0.9091	4,546
Year 2	4,000	0.8264	3,306
Year 3	3,000	0.7513	2,254
Year 4	2,000	0.6830	1,366
Net present value			1,472

Project B generates a much higher profit than project A. This could be expected because as shown above it requires no net investment after its payback in year 3.

When interpreting the NPV the simple rules are that positive is good – there is a surplus over and above the cost of funding; and that negative is bad – there is insufficient cash from the proposed project to pay for funding.

What discount rate should be applied?

The discount rate is not the current bank borrowing rate as this does not reflect that a substantial proportion of investment funds are likely to be derived from shareholders. The more appropriate rate is the weighted average cost of capital (WACC – see Chapter 3). This is a longer-term rate that takes into account the mix of funding sources including equity, loans and overdrafts.

The WACC is the rate required to meet investors' expectations. Therefore if a project delivers a positive NPV at the WACC rate it will have achieved a surplus above the minimum required by investors. However, the WACC does not allow room for risks that might create shortfalls in projects, so many businesses add a risk factor and use a risk-weighted WACC to evaluate projects. For example, a WACC rate could be around 10% but may be adjusted to 12–15% to allow for risk. If an investment yields a return below WACC, it has destroyed value and should not have been embarked upon.

Internal rate of return

Although the interpretation of NPV may be simple, with positive being good and negative being bad, this does not provide an understanding of the variations that the investment can absorb and still be viable. A good indicator is to know how high an interest rate can be tolerated before an investment will fail to make an acceptable return. With a WACC of 10%, if the highest rate at which an investment can still be profitable is only 11%, there is little room for error before it becomes value destroying. Compare this with a project that is value creating up to, say, 32%, where there is plenty of room for error and delays, and a profit is still likely.

The interest rate at which a project makes neither a profit nor a

FIG 5.5 **Net present value at different discount rates**

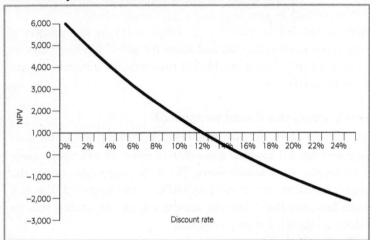

loss is known as the internal rate of return (IRR). With a project of more than two years there is no formula to calculate this rate and iteration is the only technique that can be used. Spreadsheet software programs such as Excel also use iteration to find this value.

Calculating the NPV of a project at different discount rates will identify the rate at which it becomes zero. In Figure 5.5 the NPV of project A has been plotted for a range of discount rates. The graph is a curve and therefore any linear interpolation will only be an approximation of the actual rate.

The rate for project A is 12%, meaning that it has little tolerance for errors before it would make a loss. For project B the rate is much higher at 17.8% as illustrated in Table 5.11.

Because cash flow data is a series of assumptions, there is little or no point in calculating the IRR more precisely than whole numbers.

The IRR is the primary method of investment appraisal, although most organisations use it in conjunction with the net present value to make sure that a large profitable project is not rejected in favour of a smaller project with a higher rate of return.

TABLE 5.11 **NPV of Project B at 17% and 18% discount rates**

		Discount factor 17%	Present value	Discount factor 18%	Present value
Year 0	(10,000)	1.0000	(10,000)	1.0000	(10,000)
Year 1	5,000	0.8547	4,274	0.8475	4,237
Year 2	4,000	0.7305	2,922	0.7182	2,873
Year 3	3,000	0.6244	1,873	0.6086	1,826
Year 4	2,000	0.5337	1,067	0.5158	1,032
Net present value			136		(32)

Modified internal rate of return

An IRR correctly identifies the annual return on investment on a project providing there are no interim cash flows being generated. Where interim cash flows exist the calculation assumes they can be reinvested at the IRR rate, which is unlikely to be the case. More realistically, interim cash flows are used to reduce investment capital and are therefore applied to avoid paying funding costs at the WACC rate. This actual reinvestment rate is likely to be much lower than the IRR rate, so an IRR rate that is calculated on a project with interim cash flows may well be overvalued.

The modified internal rate of return (MIRR) calculations start by taking the sum of the negative cash flows (payments) and discounts this to time zero. The future values of the positive cash flows (receipts) are found by compounding them up to the final period of the project, using a reinvestment or WACC rate. The MIRR is the rate that discounts the future values of the positive flows to match the present value of the negative flows. Many believe this to be a more realistic expectation of value from a project.

Ways of acquiring assets

A business's debt capacity (see Chapter 3) will limit the amount of capital that can be raised to fund the business without equity being issued. In turn the amount of capital available will limit the amount of cash that can be committed to the purchase of assets. Thus the amount of cash available for investment will determine a business's growth rate, requiring it to find other ways to access assets without the upfront cash cost of purchase needing to be explored.

There are two options:

- Funding strategies – leasing, including finance leases, operating leases (renting), and sale and lease back.
- Operating strategies – franchising and outsourcing.

Leasing

One of the main benefits of leasing an asset compared with ownership is that for the lessee the cash flows change from a large upfront payment to a series of smaller payments over the asset's life. In terms of the J curve profile (see Figure 5.1), the trough is much shallower. This means that less funding is required and payback can be faster. Effectively, the cash flows to obtain the asset are much more in line with the cash flows generated by using the asset. For example, the purchase price of an aircraft is, say, $100m at the outset. The aircraft may last 20 years and during that time it is hoped the cash flow from operations will fund the interest and pay down the debt. If it is purchased on a 20-year lease, the annual payment may be $7.5 million, giving it a much flatter cash flow profile.

Although the cash flow profile of a lease will be flatter, the overall cost may be higher. The lease premiums should recover for the lessor not only the cost of the asset, but also the interest on its own funding, the cost of administration and a profit on the transaction. However, an advantage may be gained in that the lessor may have a lower WACC (see Chapter 3) than the lessee, making the funding cost lower. The interest rate at which the lease is priced will include the cost of the perceived risk of the lessee, although if the lessee defaults the lessor has some protection as it will be able recover the asset and use any disposal proceeds to partially reduce its exposure.

The tax treatment of leases can be significant. Asset ownership can qualify for tax allowances, and thus in rental agreements it is the lessor who gets the tax benefits of ownership and the lessee has only the opex flow of the lease payments to use in tax computations. The precise rules vary by jurisdiction, so advice may need to be sought on the most appropriate choice.

Finance leases

These are long-term leases for the life of an asset – and usually for items that do not become technologically obsolete. They give the lessee the benefits and drawbacks of ownership, so in the financial statements they are considered as assets, and are depreciated.

Importantly, the obligation to pay future lease premiums is considered as debt in the balance sheet of the lessee and thus it is used in the calculation of gearing or leverage and in evaluating debt capacity.

International Accounting Standards provide various tests for defining finance leases, though these depend on the substance of the transaction rather than the form. These tests include whether:

- the lease transfers ownership of the asset to the lessee by the end of the lease term;
- the lessee has the option to purchase the asset at a price that is expected to be sufficiently lower than fair value at the date the option becomes exercisable, and, at the start of the lease, it is reasonably certain that the option will be exercised;
- the lease term is for the major part of the economic life of the asset, even if title is not transferred;
- at the start of the lease, the present value of the minimum lease payments amounts to the majority of the fair value of the leased asset;
- the lease assets are of a specialised nature such that only the lessee can use them without major modifications being made.

Operating leases

These are short-term leases in comparison to the asset's life – sometimes called renting. The lessee uses the asset but does not take on the benefits or drawbacks of ownership, which are retained by the lessor. The rental cost of an operating lease is considered an operating expense.

Although there is a contractual obligation to pay future lease premiums, the amounts are not shown as a liability on the balance sheet and are included only by way of a note to the accounts. This is a type of off-balance-sheet financing and is the much preferred method of leasing.

Franchising

For businesses that need a significant number of customer outlets, such as shops or restaurants, the capital required to set them up and fill them with inventory will constrain the rate of growth. A franchise model may provide an effective way to accelerate a roll out. Franchisees buy the rights to build their own outlets, which trade under the franchise brand and offer a customer experience consistent with other similarly branded outlets. The benefits of this model are not only the cash flow effects – each franchise that is sold raises its own cash – but also the fact that owner-managers are generally more motivated than employees.

Franchising only works if the business has an established brand, a track record of success and the business model is easy to replicate – for example, McDonald's and Subway restaurants. Neither business would have such a global reach if it owned all its outlets. Defined supply agreements, IT systems and other franchisee obligations can help retain a level of control and generate revenue flows back to the franchisor.

Outsourcing

This is where a process or service is contracted out to be performed by another business. Some examples are the outsourced manufacturing of components or finished goods and the supply of services such as IT or security.

The main reason for outsourcing is normally to hand over an activity to another party that can add competitive advantage. For example, the outsource business may have a lower cost base or economies of scale that enable the product or service to be provided cheaper than a business can provide them in house. Alternatively, it may offer expertise that is not available internally.

When activities are outsourced, both parties need to have realistic expectations of each other and foster an open relationship focused on effective and consistently reliable delivery.

The financial benefits are in the change of cost structure and cash flow. Usually costs for assets (depreciation) and staff are fixed (as described in Chapter 2). This means that a business needs to maintain volumes in order to generate the income to cover these costs. With outsourcing, the contract can be structured such that the product or service is purchased on a per unit basis only when required. Thus the cost becomes a variable cost, tracking volume levels and maintaining margins when sales fluctuate. In particular, it avoids having to carry a fixed cost in periods of low activity.

The cash flow benefit of outsourcing is that an asset purchase is usually avoided. Payments to the outsource business will also be made on normal terms such as 30 or 45 days after the month of invoice – that is, much later than would be the case if in-house staff were being paid to do the same work.

The outsource business is likely to be well aware of the financial and cash flow effects of its activities and will no doubt price the risks of managing these into the contract. However, where the outsource provider is supplying many businesses, economies of scale mean that it will not need to recover all its fixed costs from a single customer.

Outsourcing switches the risk from one of asset ownership and production to one of managing a third party, auditing quality and ensuring sustainability. Many companies have found that a much harder risk to manage.

Ways of releasing cash tied up in assets

Most people know only too well how easily assets can accumulate, acquired at a point of perceived need and several years later left lying idle. These inert assets may have the potential to release cash as well as space.

In a business, an asset review should be completed at least annually: for audit purposes to check their existence, but more importantly for cash purposes to review their utilisation. For unused or rarely used assets there is the potential to release cash through either their resale or, where metals are involved, their sale for scrap.

Discipline is required to apply this review regularly. Delays in application inevitably reduce any resale values.

Sale and lease back

This is an alternative way to release cash that is tied up in owned assets so it can be directed to better uses, such as investment in assets that can yield a higher return. It can also be used by a distressed business as a way to pay down mounting debts. In this situation the lease element will often be an operating lease.

An example is where a business acquired a property some years ago and a substantial gain in value has been identified. Realising this value in cash and using it to fund operating assets might be the most effective method of funding expansion. The asset is sold to a financing company or bank and at the same time a lease contract is signed so the business can continue using the asset without interruption. The business receives the full value of the property immediately in cash.

The downside of such transactions is that any legal charges over the property will have to be paid with the cash (for example, a bank that has used the property as security for a loan) before any remaining amounts can be used for other assets. Moreover, without the property in the business to provide security, the amount of available borrowing might be reduced and the increased risk might raise the interest rate charged. The capital gain that arises on the sale of the asset may also create a tax liability, though in some jurisdictions forms of roll-over relief can be used to defer this, providing the capital gain is invested back into assets.

The techniques for including the cash flows of a lease in a financial evaluation are explained above.

6 Product profitability

THERE ARE ESSENTIALLY TWO WAYS to raise long-term funds within a business without liquidating assets:

- seek external providers of finance (shareholders or banks) for which management will need to demonstrate that they have a profitable business, such that finance providers will be satisfied with their return;
- operate profitably and earn the cash from successful trading.

The first method provides cash more quickly, but both sources require a business to be fundamentally profitable if it wishes to acquire cash.

Over time profitable products or services should generate cash and unprofitable products or services will consume cash. The words "over time" are important as the cash generation effect is not instant. Normal trading involves cash being tied up in working capital (see Chapter 4), but once suppliers and operating costs have been paid and customer balances collected, a profitable product or service should result in a surplus of cash.

The revenue on a product or service needs to be able to cover not only the direct costs of its provision, but also a share of the indirect costs (such as overheads), as well as depreciation, interest on the funding of the assets and working capital committed to operating the product or service. These latter elements are more difficult to identify. But only after all these costs are considered can profitability be evaluated.

Building up the costs of a product

To be able to work out the full cost of a product or service requires an understanding of how the two main types of cost behave. Variable costs are those that change directly in proportion to volume, such as components or product packaging. Fixed costs typically stay constant in the short term for small volume changes, such as rent for a building. Each cost will typically exhibit one or other behaviour and need to be categorised as such. (See also Chapter 2.)

It is also necessary to understand the difference between direct and indirect costs in order to work out the full cost of a product.

Direct costs

These are costs that are specifically identifiable as constituents of a product or service. The majority of variable costs are direct, for example components for a product in a manufacturing business. Direct costs also include some fixed costs, such as the depreciation of the machinery used to produce the product.

Indirect costs

These are costs that do not have a connection with the provision of a product or service, for example the costs of running a canteen or site security. They are necessary to running a business as a whole, but cannot be broken down easily to identify the amount attributable to an individual product or service.

These costs are sometimes called overheads and typically cover areas such as HR (human resources), finance and IT (information technology). Although it is difficult to link them to a product or service, it is crucial that a business's products or services generate sufficient revenue to not only pay for them but also produce a profit. Many indirect costs are typically fixed, for example rent and the costs of staff within the overhead departments.

The full cost of a product or service

The full cost of a product or service will consist of three elements: the variable, direct fixed and indirect fixed costs. Each of these becomes increasingly difficult to calculate as the fixed costs need to be fairly

FIG 6.1 **Components of a full product cost**

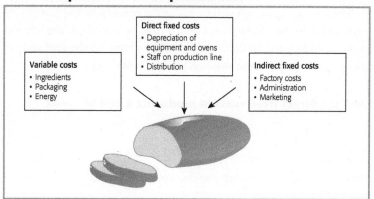

shared or apportioned across the products and services that benefit from their use. A "fair share" is a judgment that provokes arguments in businesses as the method of apportionment used can make a significant difference to the perceived profitability of a product.

It is important to note that the cost of the product or service does not determine its selling price (except in some cost-plus type contracts in businesses such as construction or engineering). The selling price is normally determined by the relative value proposition of a product or service in its market. The cost information is required to evaluate whether the market is attractive and profitable and thus worth competing in. Continuous improvement and the squeezing out of cost provide major enhancements that can either be taken as profit or used to offer a lower selling price.

Figure 6.1 illustrates how to calculate the full cost of a product. The costs of producing a loaf of bread are shown in Table 6.1.

TABLE 6.1 **Variable costs of producing a loaf of bread**

		$
Flour	0.5kg at $1 per kg	0.50
Energy		0.07
Yeast, salt and other items		0.03
Packaging	One bag	0.01
Total		**0.61**

At this stage the calculation is already inexact. For example, there will be wastage as dough will be lost in the manufacturing process – it may be left in the mixing bowl or tins may be overfilled. Therefore it is common to gross up the variable cost by a wastage element such as 3% or 5%. Reducing these wastage levels is a profit opportunity.

TABLE 6.2 **Direct fixed costs in producing a loaf of bread**

		$
Depreciation	Cost per year	12,000
Staff	One person (including employment benefits per year)	30,000
Distribution	Cost per year	8,000
Total		50,000

The total direct fixed costs are $50,000. But how much of this relates to one loaf? There are two issues: the basis of allocation and the volume denominator.

Basis of allocation

A method of allocation should be used to divide the total cost fairly across the volume of products produced. If production consists of only one type of bread, the cost can be simply divided by the number of loaves produced. However, if two different types of bread are made, such as a small granary loaf and a large white loaf, should the cost be split by weight rather than by loaf? A further complication might be that the granary loaf commands a 50% price premium, so there is an argument that the fixed costs should be split by a product's ability to pay.

There is no correct answer, as a split by loaf will allocate both loaves the same amount of direct fixed costs. This clearly gives a cost advantage to the larger loaf. Allocating by weight means the cost per kilo of each size does not reflect any economies of scale in producing larger products.

Ultimately, the method of apportionment chosen is a management decision that needs to be fair to the products and is preferably simple to apply. Trying to capture data to make the process more precise often only adds complexity and potentially even more cost in recording and using the information.

In a service industry, the number of hours of staff time spent on a job is often used as a basis of allocation.

Volume denominator

In dividing the cost by, say, the number of loaves (volume of production), which volume should be used? It could be last year's volume (which is historic), budget (which can be significantly at odds with reality) or actual (which can only be known in arrears). A realistic budget is the most common method used.

When an allocation method and a volume basis have been selected, the amount of direct fixed costs per loaf can be calculated.

TABLE 6.3 **Indirect fixed costs in producing a loaf**

	$
Factory costs	215,000
Administration	128,000
Marketing	132,000
Total	475,000

The total indirect fixed costs are $475,000. These are the costs for the whole factory, which may produce many products of many different sizes. The difficulties are not only to identify how much relates to one product but also, as with direct fixed costs, to decide on the volume denominator.

Cost apportionment

The overheads need to be split across all the products made by a business. Failure to do this could result in a business not understanding the true cost of each product and hence each product's viability in a competitive market.

The difficulty is how to attribute costs to products where the link is indeterminable, such as the cost of site security. The simplest method is to add up all the indirect fixed costs and allocate them by one of the bases mentioned under direct fixed costs, such as unit volume, weight, machine time and labour hours. Although this is a clearly identifiable method, it can dictate thinking and ultimately behaviour. For example, if costs are allocated on labour hours, products that require fewer labour hours will be deemed to have lower costs. This may encourage efficiency, but it will also encourage managers to have labour-intensive work, such as component manufacture, done outside the business to reduce their overheads.

Applying this method to the bread example, the $475,000 would be split over the number of direct production labour hours. If these are 9,500 for the whole factory, for every hour there would be:

$$\frac{\$475,000}{9,500} = \$50 \text{ of indirect fixed cost to be recovered}$$

If a member of staff earns $20 per hour, the bread staff cost of $30,000 in Table 6.2 equates to 1,500 hours. Bread would need to be responsible for 1,500 × $50 = $75,000 of indirect fixed costs. Cutting the number of staff hours to reduce the allocation of indirect costs becomes a temptation for the product's manager, but this could result in a reduction in quality, which could affect the brand value.

A more sophisticated method of allocating indirect costs is to apportion overheads to production departments (design, manufacture, quality, warehouse, dispatch, and so on), which then charge their costs to a product according to how much it draws on the time and resources of each department, thus helping make sure that each product is charged for the true cost of its manufacture. Alternatively, activity-based costing (ABC) can be used, allocating costs based on the activity or driver that caused the cost to be incurred. For example, in a warehouse the storage costs are determined by storage time and forklift truck costs are determined by the amount of product movement.

The more refined the process becomes, the more data are required and the more cost is incurred in identifying, capturing and calculating the product cost. Thus investing time in costing detail should only be done to review or rationalise the portfolio. Otherwise, it may provide interesting information, but a focus on getting value for money from each cost is often more effective.

The cost of a loaf of bread

If it is assumed that 100,000 loaves are to be made, the cost of one loaf is as shown in Table 6.4.

TABLE 6.4 **Cost of one loaf of bread**

Variable cost	Uplift by 5% for wastage	$0.61 per unit divided by 0.95	$0.64
Direct fixed cost	Assume 100,000 loaves	$50,000 divided by 100,000	$0.50
Indirect fixed costs	Assume allocated on labour hours	$75,000 divided by 100,000	$0.75
Total			$1.89

This is of course valid only for the allocation method applied and the volume of 100,000. For higher volumes the cost per loaf reduces and vice versa.

With the sales price known, the profitability of the product can be calculated.

Relevance of depreciation

Depreciation has been included under direct fixed costs for the purpose of calculating profit. Depreciation is not a cash flow and therefore the cash generated per unit would be:

Cash generated per unit = profit per unit + depreciation per unit

This calculation is effectively the EBITDA per unit (as explained in Chapter 2). This will be a higher value than profit per unit, but it has to be carefully interpreted.

When a business acquired the original asset being depreciated, it would have been funded by investors' cash, perhaps through a specific loan. Over the life of the asset the business's products need to generate sufficient cash to enable the loan to be repaid. If they do not, by the time the asset is scrapped it will be worth nothing yet the loan will still need repaying. For cash flow purposes, the inclusion of deprecation can be regarded as the capital repayment of the investment, not the wearing out of the asset. Thus a product's profitability is suitable for gauging its viability.

To ensure the true cost of funding the asset is recovered from a product, it may also be appropriate to include the funding cost (or interest element) of the cash tied up. This is done by adding an amount for interest calculated on the net book value of the fixed asset at the current WACC.

The net book value can also be increased by the working capital tied up in the production of the product covering the inventory plus the receivables less the payables. For products that take a long time to manufacture, the inventory of work in progress can be a substantial investment of cash, sometimes as much as the fixed assets. The funding cost of this total net investment in assets (both fixed and working capital) can then be calculated at the current WACC.

Analysis of this information will need to be determined as follows. If the funding cost is ignored:

$$\frac{\text{Product profitability before interest}}{\text{Net assets (fixed assets + working capital)}} \% > \text{WACC}\%$$

This is a simple ROI percentage calculation where the numerator is EBIT (earnings before interest and tax) divided by the net assets required for its production. It is derived from the product profitability calculation explained above including the cost of the depreciation. If the funding cost is included:

$$\text{Product profitably} - (\text{WACC} \times \text{net assets}) > 0$$

This is a value calculation. The WACC is the rate required to keep the pool of investors satisfied. Therefore the WACC multiplied by the net assets will be the minimum return required to justify the investment in the net assets required. The product profitability minus the required return needs to be greater than zero to create value. A value of less than zero means that value is being destroyed and the product cannot generate sufficient surplus to provide investors with their required return.

The product portfolio

Should a product fail to show a profit using the methods described above, its elimination may not improve business performance. The difficulty is the indirect fixed costs. If a product is removed, many of the indirect fixed costs, such as site security, HR and IT, will not change.

It would also be unwise to eliminate a product based on one year of poor performance. What is required is a full business case (see Chapter 5) to evaluate the impact on the whole business of the removal of a product over, say, five years. This will take into account the lost revenue, the saved direct costs and the limited (if any) change in indirect costs.

7   Cash surpluses

THIS CHAPTER COVERS OPTIONS for dealing with substantial cash surpluses – a situation that many businesses never achieve.

As explained in Chapter 1, the aim of a business is to produce a sustainable superior return on investment. Excess cash should be either reinvested or returned to investors on the principle of it either "earning" or "returning". For most businesses any surplus cash that is generated will be reinvested in funding expansionary or replacement assets and/or distributed as a dividend. The principles in this chapter apply when the surplus cash far exceeds the amount needed for these purposes with a time horizon of at least a year in view. The longer-term existence of the cash surplus is important as surpluses may be created and consumed ordinarily in a business, especially a seasonal business. The longer term is where the cash flow forecast shows that the surplus will exist above and beyond any predicted utilisation.

When a business is generating substantial amounts of surplus cash and has little debt, investors can rightly challenge management to raise its ambitions for growth either organically or through acquisition. However, the criteria for investment described in Chapter 5 should be no less ruthlessly applied in times of spare cash than they would be in times of scarce cash. Investment opportunities or acquisitions taken at premium prices can simply destroy investors' capital or provide low or diluting returns. Just because cash is available at one moment does not mean appropriate investment opportunities are available at the same time. In such circumstances, holding the surplus cash in accessible form will enable opportunities to be pursued when it becomes advantageous to do so.

FIG 7.1 **Options for managing surplus cash**

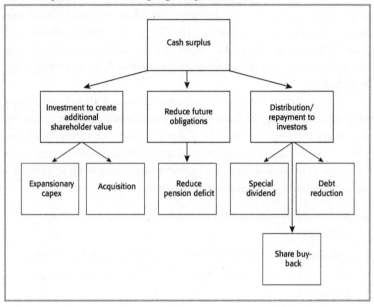

If no suitable investment opportunities are available, the options for managing the surplus cash are to:

■ reduce future obligations such as pension deficits;

■ pay down debt;

■ distribute to equity investors (through either a special dividend or a share buy-back).

This is summarised in Figure 7.1.

Investments to create additional shareholder value

This is covered in Chapter 5 where the cash flow evaluation of opportunities is explored.

Reduce pension deficits

In recent years many businesses that had established their own company pension schemes with defined employee benefits have found them to be underfunded. This is where the net present value of the expected liabilities to the current and future pensioners exceeds the net present value of the expected future investment returns and contributions. Typically, the reason is a combination of increasing life expectancy and lower investment returns than were originally anticipated.

Where a deficit has occurred in a pension fund, a business has an obligation to top up the fund should its performance fail to create the necessary amounts to close the gap and meet those future liabilities. These pension liabilities are shown on the balance sheet as long-term liabilities or provisions and management is responsible for instigating a deficit-reduction programme. Some deficit-reduction methods are:

- increasing pension contributions from members and the company;
- reducing benefit entitlements to existing and future pensioners;
- raising the age of retirement to delay the commencement of payments;
- changing the investment strategy, either investing more aggressively to try to achieve enhanced returns (but this has downside risks) or switching to fixed-interest returns to avoid market volatility of the investment portfolio.

Another option is to use surplus cash that could be applied to debt reduction to reduce the pension deficit. The benefit is that the interest on the borrowings is tax deductible in the business, whereas the interest earned on the funds deposited in the scheme is tax free. For example, if debt cost 6% and tax rates were 30%, the actual cost to investors of the debt is 4.2%. If the cash can be invested in the pension scheme with a return of 5% or more, the interest differential will help close the pension deficit.

This is a permanent option as the cash deposited in the scheme cannot be taken out if the business experiences a cash shortage in the future. However, both the deposited cash and the interest differential assist in closing the deficit gap.

It is worth noting that investment analysts typically characterise pension deficits as debt when assessing the gearing or leverage of a business, so the use of cash to repay debt or reduce a pension deficit is unlikely to make any difference to the gearing or leverage levels for evaluating financing capacity (as explained in Chapter 3).

Pay down debt

Reducing debt may seem an obvious way of using surplus cash, especially for people who are lucky enough to be in such a position in their personal lives, but it is not necessarily the best option for the creation of shareholder value in a business. In terms of funding costs, debt is likely to have a lower cost of capital than some of the other sources of finance, particularly when the tax relief on the interest is taken into account. A repayment of debt will also disturb the leverage or gearing ratios. This will change the WACC for the whole business and potentially affect the funding costs of others types of finance (see Chapter 3).

The most important principle is therefore to pay down the funding source with the highest cost to the shareholder and end up with a lower WACC at the completion of any repayment process.

As the graph in Chapter 3 (Figure 3.4) shows, the optimum leverage or gearing level is around 50% for many businesses. Therefore the starting point for any return of capital is to identify whether an advantage can be gained by reducing debt, equity or a combination of the two. The nearer the optimum mix of funding sources, the lower the WACC will become and thus the greater the shareholder value derived from the activities to which the funds have been applied.

For businesses with leverage or gearing levels below 40%, the most effective use for the cash may be a distribution to equity investors (see below). This will reduce equity, and providing that leverage or gearing levels remain below 50% after the distribution it will also reduce WACC. Where businesses have leverage or gearing above 60%, the most effective use of cash is most likely to be debt reduction. This will take the debt level towards or below 50% of the total funds, thus improving the business's credit status or credit rating and over time reducing interest rates on the remaining debt. Enhanced debt status will also reduce equity investors' required return and in combination with the reduced debt returns yield an overall reduced WACC.

If a business decides that debt reduction is the best option, it then needs to consider which type of debt it would be most suitable to repay.

Stage one: look at medium-term debt requirements

A medium-term cash flow forecast can be drawn up to reveal the profile of maturing debt and additional debt-raising expectations. This will show any repayment opportunities over the next few months that may absorb much of the cash surplus without an accelerated debt repayment. It would be foolish to make a repayment if there are likely to be additional debt-raising requirements within a short time.

If there is a clear cash surplus after this analysis, a prepayment or repayment is justified.

Stage two: evaluate the funding cost of debt elements
Annual cost

All forms of debt should be ranked in order of their annual cost. Cost is not necessarily just the interest cost alone. In the case of an overdraft, there may be facility and non-utilisation fees that enhance the overall annual cost.

Penalty clauses

The prepayment of debt can attract penalty clauses from the provider and thus part of the repayment benefit will be lost. Hence it might be more advantageous to repay a lower-interest-rate debt than a higher-rate one with a penalty clause. Finding the true cost of debt where fees and penalties are involved requires a discounted cash flow analysis. The cash flows need to be identified and then the IRR calculated (see Chapter 5).

For example, two-year debt at 8% cannot easily be compared with two-year debt at 9% with a 1.5% penalty clause. If the debt sum is $1m, the true cost of the second scenario can be calculated as follows (interest paid annually in arrears).

9% debt with 1.5% penalty clause

By calculating the IRR of the total cash flow line the overall saving per year of repaying this debt is 8.16%, so it is more advantageous to repay this debt rather than the debt at 8%.

TABLE 7.1 **Cash flow, $'000**

Time	0	1	2	
Penalty	(15)	–	–	(15)
Interest	–	90	90	180
Capital	(1,000)	–	1,000	0
Total	(1,015)	90	1,090	165

For debt instruments with more frequent interest payments a more detailed analysis, such as quarterly or monthly, will be required.

Yield to maturity

Where debt has been raised in the form of bonds, the coupon rate may not be the actual rate that an investor gets or the rate that could be saved by a business if the bonds are bought back today. For example, a $100 5% bond with three years to maturity may trade at $95. This means that investors get not only the 5% yield but also the growth in capital from $95 to $100. The true yield to maturity of the bond has to be calculated in the same way as the example above using the IRR (see Table 7.2).

TABLE 7.2 **Yield to maturity**

Time	0	1	2	3	
Capital	(95)	–	–	100	5
Interest	–	5	5	5	15
Total	(95)	5	5	105	20

The IRR of the cash flows or the overall yield to maturity is 6.92%, which would make this debt more worthwhile to redeem than bank debt at 6.5%.

It is important to consider dealing and other costs such as stamp duty. The debt may trade at $95, but when the acquisition costs of buying the debt in the market are included the overall yield will fall. Acquisition costs should be included in the calculation to ensure yields are accurately compared and cash is used appropriately.

The benefit of bond redemption is that it can be spread over a period of time. A broker can be instructed to buy back the debt whenever the price falls below a certain value, which means that the yield benefit has a floor. There may be times during the period of buy-back when additional yield can be gained if the bond price falls below the target price. The process can also be stopped, providing some flexibility should new investment opportunities emerge. However, if the market becomes aware that a business is buying back its own bonds, investors may start to take an interest and there may then be fewer opportunities to buy at the target price or below.

Stage three: select the debt to repay

Before making a repayment it is worth studying market data and to compare the interest-rate environment for existing debt with what it may be when future debt needs to be raised. If a business has low-fixed-rate debt taken out in a low-interest-rate environment, it would be unwise to repay it if new debt is likely to be required in the short term at a much higher rate.

The most expensive debt is likely to be the most advantageous to repay. However, as the most expensive debt is likely to have the most flexible terms, such as an overdraft, its removal from the pool of sources of finance will leave the business without an emergency buffer to cover any short-term deficits. Thus the retention of an overdraft facility is likely to be crucial in liquidity planning, although clearing any deficit balance would certainly be a priority. Obviously if a business is planning the appropriate allocation of a substantial cash surplus, it is unlikely to be running an overdraft at the time of making a repayment decision.

In conclusion, if debt is to be redeemed or repaid prematurely, it should be the debt that is carrying the highest cost to maturity, providing this will not lead to higher-rate debt being taken on in the foreseeable future.

Distribution or repayment to investors

A distribution to investors will reduce excess capital. The two main ways of doing this are through a special dividend or a share buy-back. When selecting the most appropriate method, it important to consider the significant differences in the costs and benefits for investors.

Special dividend

This is a distribution of profit by means of a payment of a fixed amount per share. Dividends are regarded as income for investors. They are subject to taxation in the year of payment and will potentially attract income tax at the investor's highest rate. This may encourage some investors to sell their shares cum dividend (with dividend rights) so that the value of the dividend is included in the share price. The effect of this sale is to crystallise a capital gain or loss rather than income, which in some jurisdictions is taxed at a lower rate.

Share buy-back

This is when a company buys its own shares on the market. The benefit is that the value of any shares remaining on the market should increase, as the earnings will be distributed between fewer investors. Investors will benefit from a gain, but it will not be subject to tax until their shareholding is sold, which may be many years later. Any capital gains tax that arises after various reliefs may also be chargeable at a lower rate than the income tax rate. An example is as follows:

- A company has a market capitalisation of $12m (calculated by taking 6m shares in issue, trading at a price of $2; or a price/earnings (PE) ratio of 12 and earnings of $1m).

- It has a cash surplus of $2m in a deposit account earning 2%, which is taxed at 30%. Management decides to use this cash to buy back shares.

- When the cash is spent, the company's earnings fall from $1m to $972,000 as a consequence of removing the $28,000 of taxed interest being earned. The number of shares falls from 6m to 5m as the company buys back 1m at the current share price.

- The market capitalisation or value of the company becomes $11.664m (calculated by taking the revised earnings of $972,000 and multiplying by the same PE ratio of 12). Dividing the new value of the company by 5m (the number of shares remaining) gives a share value of $2.33, a 16.5% increase.

The assumption in this example is that all 1m shares can be bought back at a price of $2. In reality, the removal of 16% of the shares is likely to push up the share price during the buy-back process, so $2m will buy fewer than 1m shares. As in the bond buy-back described above, the transaction is unlikely to be completed in one deal, so a broker will have to be instructed to buy a volume of stock at any price up to a maximum set price.

Furthermore, the company's P/E ratio may not stay the same. Earnings from the company's activities may be unchanged by the transaction, but investors may have expected the surplus cash to be used for expansion and growth rather than repayment so the P/E ratio may fall.

It is possible to pay too much for shares during a buy-back – as it is during the takeover or acquisition of another company – by buying them when the P/E ratio is unusually high. As with most share trading, the timing and price are critical to the success of the transaction. Placing a blanket order to buy below a set price means that the required volume of stock may not be acquired if the stock rarely falls below the set price. Consequently, the surplus cash may not be fully utilised. This would be the right conclusion, as it is better to carry surplus cash than to pay too much for stock and decrease value for the remaining investors.

When shares are bought back they are kept off the market, but they can be reissued should there be a need to raise cash in the future. However, if the shares are bought back when the business is riding high and the P/E ratio is strong, and then cash is needed when the business is less successful and the P/E ratio lower, the share sale price could well be lower than the share buy-back cost.

Having surplus cash to distribute sounds good in theory, but it can be a problem. For example, when oil prices are high, oil companies find themselves in this situation. In 2008, when the oil price peaked at over $140 a barrel, many large oil companies accumulated cash amounting to over a quarter of their balance sheet. Although overall returns were high, investors rightly criticised the lack of return being achieved on so much of the balance sheet. In the absence of investment opportunities, they undertook substantial buy-backs of their own shares. Subsequently, oil prices fell and so did the earnings and share prices. Therefore with hindsight they overpaid for their buy-backs.

Glossary

Cross references are in **bold**.

Accrual	A type of **payable** where the products or services have been received in one accounting period, but the invoicing and payment take place in a subsequent accounting period.
Activity-based costing (ABC)	The allocation of **indirect costs** to products or services in proportion to the activities that drove the cost to be incurred.
Amortisation	The writing off of an **intangible asset** over a period.
Apportionment	The spreading of **overheads** across various cost centres as part of calculating the cost of a product or service.
Asset	Something owned or controlled that has a future economic benefit.
Asset finance	A loan secured on **receivables, inventory** or property.
Balance sheet	A statement at a specified date showing the financial position of a business in terms of its **assets, liabilities** and shareholders' funds (**equity**). Also known as a statement of financial position.
Borrowing capacity	The amount of finance a business is able to raise

Borrowing facility	An agreed amount of borrowing that can be drawn down as required.
Bond	Fixed-interest **debt** issued in the form of a tradable security.
Bonus issue	Shares issued to existing shareholders in proportion to their existing shareholding at no charge.
Business case	The evaluation of an investment opportunity.
Capital expenditure (capex)	The purchase of **fixed assets**, typically requiring justification with a business case.
Cash	Ready money usually held in a bank account.
Cash flow	The receipts and payments of cash over a period of time.
Cash flow forecast	The prediction and timing of future cash flows.
Cash flow statement	A statement showing the funds generated by the operations and funds from other sources. It also indicates how funds have been applied and whether there is a net surplus or deficiency.
Cash pooling	The aggregation of bank balances.
Collateral	**Assets** that are pledged as security for **loans** or other credit.
Common stock	US term for **ordinary shares**.
Convertible bond	A security that is issued as a **bond** but on maturity can be converted to **equity**, providing the share price has achieved certain growth expectations.
Contingency	A reserve held to fund unforeseen events.
Cost of capital	See **weighted average cost of capital**.
Credit	A term used to describe borrowings.

Credit criteria	The conditions on which borrowings are granted, also known as lending criteria.
Credit crunch	A contraction in available credit combined with more demanding credit criteria.
Credit rating	A risk evaluation to determine creditworthiness.
Creditors	A UK term for **payables**.
Current assets	The short-term operating **assets**, including **inventory**, **receivables**, short-term investments, bank and cash balances.
Current liabilities	The **liabilities** arising as a consequence of trade, including **payables** and bank overdrafts.
Debenture	A loan secured on **assets** that is usually issued at a fixed rate of interest and repayable on a specific date.
Debtors	A UK term for **receivables**.
Debts	Amounts owed to loan providers.
Depreciation	An accounting estimate that takes account of the diminution in value of a **fixed asset** and spreads its cost over the expected useful life of the asset.
Derivative	A financial instrument where the value is derived from the difference in a range of variables applied to a notional amount of principal; examples include swaps and **options**.
Direct costs	Costs such as raw materials specifically used in the creation of a product or service.
Direct debit	An automated collection of a **receivable**. The withdrawal is initiated by the recipient under authority given by the customer.
Discounted cash flow	A technique used to value future cash flows (see **time value of money, net present value** and **internal rate of return**).

Dividend	The distribution in cash of company profits to shareholders.
Drawdown	The receipt of cash utilising a pre-arranged borrowing facility.
Earnings	The profit available to shareholders after all costs including interest and taxation.
EBITDA	Earnings before interest, tax, **depreciation** and **amortisation** – an approximation for the cash generated by a business.
Equity	Also known as shareholders' funds, or net worth, it is the sum of issued share capital (nominal value plus any premium on issue) and reserves.
Facility	See **borrowing facility**.
Factoring	The process of letting another party assume responsibility for collecting **receivables**.
Finance lease	A long-term contract for the use of an **asset**.
Fixed assets	The book value of a business's infrastructure consisting of **tangible assets**, such as property, plant and equipment, fixtures and fittings, and **intangible assets**, such as **goodwill** and brands.
Fixed charge	The security provided for a debt that is tied to a specific **asset** or group of assets.
Fixed costs	Costs that are unaffected by small changes in the level of business activity.
Forward rate agreement (FRA)	A **derivative** to determine the interest rate to be paid on a loan that will drawn down at a future date.
Franchising	The licensing of a business model and brand to franchisees who benefit from the existing reputation in building their own outlet.

Free cash flow	The cash available after all operating costs, interest, tax and SIB (stay in business) capital expenditure have been deducted; the money available to fund expansion or reward inventors.
Gearing	A UK term for **leverage**.
Goodwill	The difference between the amount paid for a company and the fair value of the net **assets** acquired.
Hedging	The use of financial structures and **derivatives** to mitigate adverse market movements in interest or foreign exchange rates.
Impairment review	A review of **fixed assets** to identify any permanent diminution in value
Income statement	A statement of revenue and costs, also known as a profit and loss account.
Indirect costs	Costs or overheads incurred in running a business that are not directly attributable to a product or service.
Initial public offering (IPO)	The widening of the shareholder base by the existing owners through selling shares and listing the company on a stock exchange.
Intangible assets	Assets that have no physical form, such as brands and patents.
Internal rate of return (IRR)	The average rate of return achieved over the life of a project, calculated by finding the discount rate where the sum of the **discounted cash flows** minus the capital outlay is equal to zero.
Inventory	Goods available for sale, including raw materials, **work in progress** and finished goods. Inventory is valued at the lower of cost or market value.
Leasing	See **finance lease** and **operating lease**.
Letter of credit	A payment guarantee from a customer's bank that is used in international trade.

Leverage	The proportion of investment provided to a company by its shareholders compared with the proportion of investment provided by other sources, which usually bears interest. High leverage (gearing) means there is a high proportion of debt.
Liability	A claim on a business as a result of a past transaction or event.
Liquidity	In business: the amount of cash and other **assets** that can be easily turned into cash (liquidated). In markets: the tradability of a security.
Loan covenant	A contractual restriction placed upon a borrower.
Loans	Borrowings, typically from a bank.
Market capitalisation	The market value of shares multiplied by the number of shares issued. This is the value of the company.
Maturity ladder	A date-ordered list of borrowings due for repayment.
Modified internal rate of return (MIRR)	An **internal rate of return** calculated with the positive cash flows reinvested at the **weighted average cost of capital.**
Net present value (NPV)	The sum of the future cash flows discounted at the cost of capital minus the capital outlay.
Operating expenditure (opex)	The cost of day-to-day items such as payroll, rent, marketing, distribution and so on.
Operating lease	A short-term contract for the use of an asset.
Option	The right, but not the obligation, to buy (for a call option) or sell (for a put option) an **asset** at a future date.

Ordinary shares	Shares that are entitled to the profits after all other costs. The US term is common stock.
Overdraft	A short-term highly flexible bank borrowing, typically within a pre-arranged facility.
Overheads	The costs of running a business rather than providing its products and services; for example, human resources, finance and building maintenance.
Payables	Amounts owing to suppliers, usually payable within one year.
Payback period	The time taken for the cash receipts from a project to exceed the cash payments. This is normally expressed in years.
Payment	An outflow of cash.
Pension deficit	A liability to a pension scheme where the **net present value** of the expected **liabilities** to the current and future pensioners exceeds the net present value of the expected future investment returns and contributions.
Price/earnings ratio (P/E)	The share price divided by the last reported earnings per share. The p/e is a multiple that shows the number of years' earnings the market values a company's shares at.
Profit	Surplus of revenue less costs.
Profit and loss account	See **income statement**.
Provision	An estimated amount to cover an expected **liability** even if the exact amount or timing of the liability is uncertain.
Receipt	An inflow of cash.
Receivables	Amounts owed to a company by its customers and usually collectable within one year.

Residual value	The anticipated value of a **fixed asset** at the end of its useful life.
Retained earnings	A company's accumulated undistributed income, also known as revenue reserves.
Return on investment (ROI)	Operating income expressed as a percentage of the investment used to earn that income.
Revenue	Income receivable from selling products or services, net of sales taxes. Revenue is reported in the **income statement**.
Rights issue	An issue of ordinary shares to existing shareholders who have a right to a number of new shares in proportion to their existing holding. The new shares are normally issued at a price below the current trading price.
Scrip issue	See **bonus issue**.
Securitisation	The creation and issuance of of tradable securities that are backed by the income generated by a portfolio of **assets** (such as **receivables**).
Share premium	The difference between the price paid for a share and its nominal value.
Shareholder value	The generation of an investment return greater than the **weighted average cost of capital**.
Shareholders' funds	A term for **equity**.
Statement of financial position	See **balance sheet**.
Stock	A UK term for **inventory**. In the US, the term is used to describe share capital (see **common stock**).
Sunk costs	Costs that have already been spent and will not change as result of making a decision.

Syndicated loan	A large loan that is provided by a group of funders (typically banks) rather than an individual institution.
Tangible assets	Assets with a physical form, such as property, plant and equipment.
Time value of money	A concept used in **discounted cash flow** analysis. Cash flows in the future are less valuable than those today.
Treasury management	Long-term cash planning including cash forecasts, development of funding lines and investment strategies.
Turnover	A term for sales or **revenue**.
Variable costs	Costs that vary in proportion to the volume of activity.
Vendor managed inventory (VMI)	The process of letting a supplier have responsibility to replenish inventory on your site.
Venture capital	Money provided to start-up businesses with high growth potential. The high risk of such ventures means that investors require management involvement and set performance criteria.
Weighted average cost of capital (WACC)	The average return that is required by investors in the business.
Work in progress	Goods in the process of being manufactured. The value of work in progress is based on the materials and labour invested.
Working capital	The sum of **inventory** plus **receivables** minus **payables**.

Index